T0126987

SIERRA
WILDFLOWERS
A Hiker's Guide

Written and illustrated by

JOHN MUIR LAWS

Foreword by Joe Medeiros

Heyday, Berkeley, California

Sierra College Press, Rocklin, California

Copyright © 2019 by John Muir Laws

All rights reserved. No portion of this work may be repro-
duced or transmitted in any form or by any means, electronic
or mechanical, including photocopying and recordings, or by
any information storage or retrieval system, without permis-
sion in writing from Heyday.

Library of Congress Control Number: 2018957710

On the front cover: Subalpine Shooting Star
On the back cover: Common Madia
Cover Design: Ashley Ingram

Published by Heyday
P.O. Box 9145, Berkeley, California 94709
(510) 549-3564
heydaybooks.com

Printed in China by Imago

10 9 8 7 6 5 4 3 2

White-Cream Flowers
pages 4–35

Red-Pink Flowers
pages 36–53

Orange Flowers
pages 54–57

Yellow Flowers
pages 58–81

Green Flowers
pages 82–83

Blue-Purple Flowers
pages 84–105

Foreword

California's signature mountain range displays an annual riot of color. From showy fields of poppies, lupines, and paintbrushes in the foothills to half-hidden orchids, lilies, and primroses in the higher meadows of our national parks, the Sierra Nevada is one of the state's premier wildflower destinations.

Most people associate wildflowers with spring, but in the Sierra they can be found from late winter through late fall. One of the benefits of a mountainous landscape is if you miss a wildflower display at lower elevation, all you have to do is travel uphill to catch the next act. In spring, the foothills are rich with palette-like displays of wildflowers in grasslands and open, sunny spaces between woodland oaks. Later in the spring and into early summer, drive up into the mountains for fewer but equally showy splashes of color in our conifer-dominated forests. By late summer and early fall, when we seek even higher ground and cooler temperatures, we'll find more flowers not only at sub-alpine elevations but also in Lilliputian gardens at the highest alpine elevations.

Sierra Wildflowers: A Hiker's Guide, which includes illustrations lovingly painted from life, is conveniently arranged by flower color and shape and includes most of the common species that you will encounter. Adapted from naturalist John Muir Laws's bestselling *The Laws Field Guide to the Sierra Nevada* (Heyday, 2007), this book features fully updated plant names as of the time of printing. (My thanks to my colleague Shawna Martinez for her assistance in this endeavor. For the most up-to-date names, please consult cnps.org or calflora.org.)

So, grab your backpack and this handy field guide and head for the hills. Just please don't pick the flowers you find—leave them for others to enjoy!

Happy Trails!—Joe Medeiros, professor emeritus of botany at Sierra College and series editor of Sierra College Press, 2019

About Sierra College Press

The Sierra College Press endeavors to reach beyond the library, laboratory, and classroom to promote and examine the Sierra Nevada. For more information, please visit www.sierracollege.edu/press.

Board of Directors: Chris Benn, Rebecca Bocchicchio, Sean Booth, Keely Carroll, Kerrie Cassidy, Mandy Davies, Dan DeFoe, David Dickson, Tom Fillebrown, Christine Freeman, Rebecca Gregg, Brian Haley, Rick Heide, Jay Hester, David Kuchera, Joe Medeiros (Editor-in-Chief), Lynn Medeiros, Sue Michaels, Gary Noy, Bart O'Brien, Sabrina Pape (Board Chair), Mike Price, Jennifer Skillen, Barbara Vineyard, and Randy White.

SIERRA COLLEGE PRESS

Acknowledgments

Many of the watercolor paintings in this book were created in the company of my father, Robert H. Laws (1930–2018). He was there when I painted the first flower (Water Cress) and the last (Sugar Stick). He spent hours keying out plants, reviewing and editing my work, and maintaining a database of completed drawings. His love, encouragement, and inspiration are with me always.

I thank the extraordinary naturalist David Lukas for his friendship, extensive field work, and review. In creating this book, I consulted some of the best naturalists in the country, and was helped and encouraged by a community of supporters, advisors, editors, and friends, without whose help this volume would not be possible. Any errors in this book are my own. With deepest regret and apologies for the inevitable inadvertent omissions, I thank Dr. Frank Almeda, Julie Carville, Ann Caudle, Josiah Clark, Leigh Davenport, Michael Ellis, Kristin Jakob, Jenny Keller, Dr. Roland Knapp, Larry Lavendel, Beatrice C. Laws, James C. Laws, Malcolm Margolin, Shawna Martinez, Dr. Joseph McBride, Joe Medeiros, Steve Medley, Moose Mutlow, Dr. Robert Patterson, Kurt Rademacher, Allan Ridley, Tom Santos, John-Austin Saviano, Dr. Arnold Schultz, Marilyn Smulyan, Jim Steele, Dr. Scott Stine, Patricia Wakida, Erik Westerlund, and Karen Wiese.

I acknowledge with great thanks the help and support of the Richard and Rhoda Goldman Fund, Boy Scout Troop 14 of San Francisco, Bureau of Land Management, California Native Plant Society, FedEx Kinko's, Gordon and Betty Moore Foundation, Hi-Tec Sports USA, Imaginova Corp., Jepson Herbarium, L. J. and Mary C. Skaggs Foundation, MACadam Computer Inc., San Francisco State University and its Sierra Nevada field campus, Sierra College, U.S. Forest Service, U.S. National Park Service, UniSense Foundation, and the Yosemite Institute.

Yours in nature,

John Muir Laws

Key to Wildflowers

Locate a plant by browsing by color or by using the key below (starting with A and AA). Focus on plant structure, as many plants which change color over the season are not shown in all their colors. Some species may have variable numbers of petals on different flowers, so look at several plants and flowers before starting.

A. **Bilaterally symmetrical** flowers: flowers can only be divided into similar halves along one central axis.

White: Go to ⊛, pages 4-9.

Red/Pink: Go to ⊛, pages 37-40.

Orange: Go to ⊛, page 55.

Yellow: Go to ⊛, pages 59-62.

Green: Go to ⊛, page 82.

Blue/Purple: Go to ⊛, pages 85-95.

AA. **Radially symmetrical** flowers: flowers can be divided into similar halves along more than one axis. Go to B and BB below.

B. Flowers in a **dense clump**, making it difficult to tell the number of petals.

White: Go to ⊙, pages 10-14.

Red/Pink: Go to ⊙, pages 41-42.

Yellow: Go to ⊙, pages 63-66.

Green: Go to ⊙, page 83.

Blue/Purple: Go to ⊙, page 96.

BB. Flowers not in a dense clump, you can count the number of petals per flower. Go to C below.

C. **3 petals**

White: Go to ③, pages 18-19.

Red/Pink: Go to ③, page 43.

Yellow: Go to ③, page 67.

Blue/Purple: Go to ③, page 97.

4 petals	White:	Go to (4), pages 16-17.
	Red/Pink:	Go to 4, pages 43-44.
	Orange:	Go to 4, page 55.
	Yellow:	Go to 4, pages 67-68.
	Green:	Go to 4, page 83.
	Blue/Purple:	Go to 4, page 98.

5 petals	White:	Go to (5), pages 18-30.
	Red/Pink:	Go to 5, pages 45-51.
	Orange:	Go to 5, page 56.
	Yellow:	Go to 5, pages 69-72.
	Green:	Go to 5, page 83.
	Blue/Purple:	Go to 5, pages 98-102.

6 petals	White:	Go to (6), pages 31-33.
	Red/Pink:	Go to 6, page 52.
	Orange:	Go to 6, page 57.
	Yellow:	Go to 6, page 73.
	Green:	Go to 6, page 83.
	Blue/Purple:	Go to 6, pages 102-103.

Many petals or plants with variable numbers of petals on different flowers. This includes daisy- or sunflower-shaped plants.

	White:	Go to (M), pages 34-35.
	Red/Pink:	Go to M, pages 52-53.
	Yellow:	Go to M, pages 74-81.
	Blue/Purple:	Go to M, pages 104-105.

White Flower Key

Choose among the groups (starting with A and AA) and follow the directions. Some species may have variable numbers of petals on different flowers, so look at several plants and flowers before starting to identify a plant.

A. Bilaterally symmetrical flowers: flowers can only be divided into similar halves along one central axis.

Go to , pages 4 (below)-9.

AA. Radially symmetrical flowers: flowers can be divided into similar halves along more than one axis. Go to B and BB below.

B. Flowers in a dense clump, making it difficult to tell the number of petals.

Go to , pages 10-14.

BB. Flowers not in a dense clump; you can count the number of petals per flower. Go to C below.

C. 3 petals: Go to ③, pages 15-16.

4 petals: Go to ④, pages 16-17.

5 petals: Go to ⑤, pages 18-30.

6 petals: Go to ⑥, pages 31-33.

Many petals or plants with variable numbers of petals on different flowers. This includes daisy- or sunflower-shaped plants.
Go to Ⓜ, pages 34-35.

dense spiral of flowers

petals fused into tube

Hooded Ladies Tresses
Spiranthes romanzoffiana
Orchidaceae
wet meadows

Orchids and Fungi

Orchids parasitize soil fungi to obtain water, nutrients, and sometimes sugars.

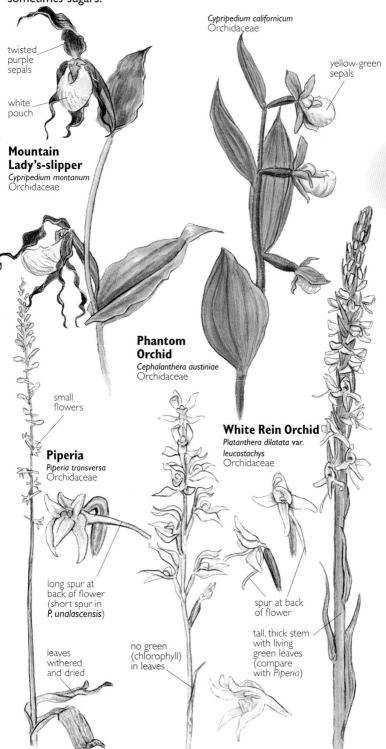

twisted purple sepals

white pouch

Mountain Lady's-slipper
Cypripedium montanum
Orchidaceae

Cypripedium californicum
Orchidaceae

yellow-green sepals

Phantom Orchid
Cephalanthera austiniae
Orchidaceae

small flowers

Piperia
Piperia transversa
Orchidaceae

long spur at back of flower (short spur in *P. unalascensis*)

leaves withered and dried

White Rein Orchid
Platanthera dilatata var. *leucostachys*
Orchidaceae

spur at back of flower

no green (chlorophyll) in leaves

tall, thick stem with living green leaves (compare with *Piperia*)

Doctrine of Signatures

It was once thought that plant shapes signified medicinal uses. Walnuts were believed to help the brain. Violets, with their heart-shaped leaves, were thought to help the heart or blood.

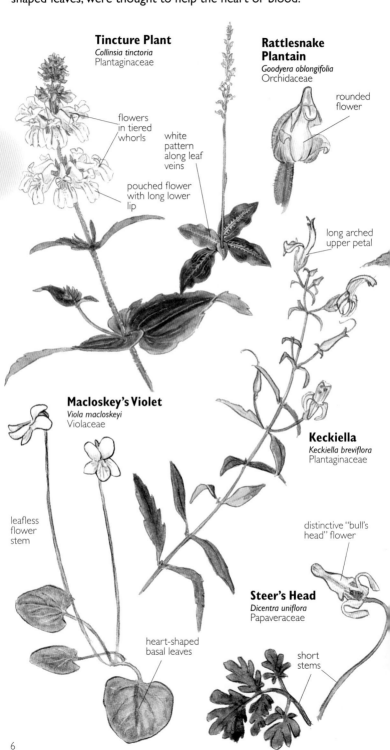

Tincture Plant
Collinsia tinctoria
Plantaginaceae

flowers in tiered whorls

white pattern along leaf veins

pouched flower with long lower lip

Rattlesnake Plantain
Goodyera oblongifolia
Orchidaceae

rounded flower

long arched upper petal

Macloskey's Violet
Viola macloskeyi
Violaceae

leafless flower stem

heart-shaped basal leaves

Keckiella
Keckiella breviflora
Plantaginaceae

distinctive "bull's head" flower

Steer's Head
Dicentra uniflora
Papaveraceae

short stems

Square Stems and Opposite Leaves: Mint Family
Many mint species have a strong and pleasant odor.

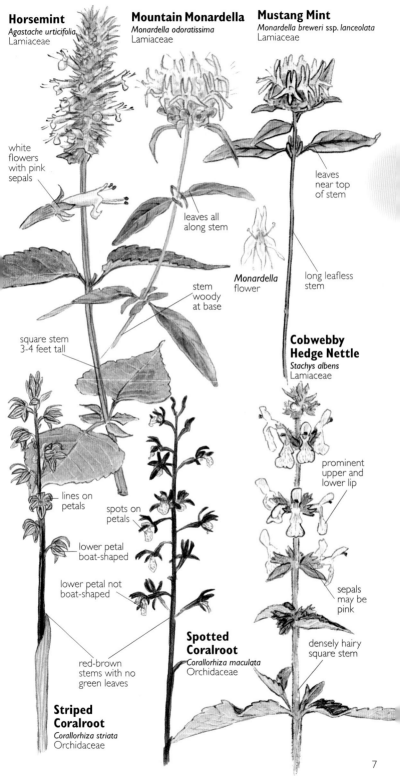

Horsemint
Agastache urticifolia
Lamiaceae

Mountain Monardella
Monardella odoratissima
Lamiaceae

Mustang Mint
Monardella breweri ssp. *lanceolata*
Lamiaceae

white flowers with pink sepals

leaves all along stem

leaves near top of stem

Monardella flower

stem woody at base

long leafless stem

square stem 3-4 feet tall

Cobwebby Hedge Nettle
Stachys albens
Lamiaceae

lines on petals

spots on petals

prominent upper and lower lip

lower petal boat-shaped

lower petal not boat-shaped

sepals may be pink

red-brown stems with no green leaves

Spotted Coralroot
Corallorhiza maculata
Orchidaceae

densely hairy square stem

Striped Coralroot
Corallorhiza striata
Orchidaceae

Poison Petals

Monkshood contains the poisonous alkaloid aconitine, which helps protect it from herbivores. This species usually has deep purple flowers (see page 85).

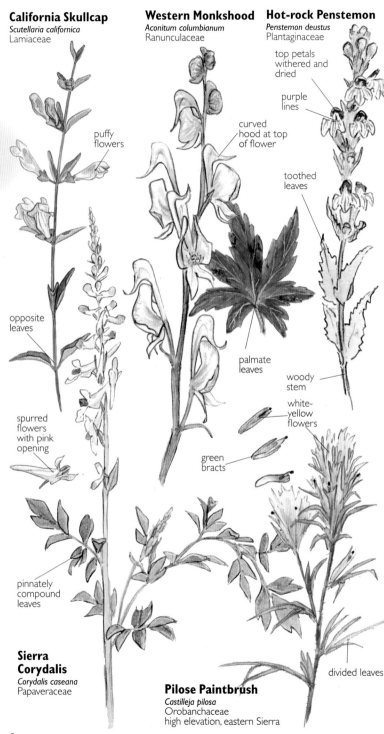

California Skullcap
Scutellaria californica
Lamiaceae

puffy flowers

opposite leaves

spurred flowers with pink opening

Western Monkshood
Aconitum columbianum
Ranunculaceae

curved hood at top of flower

palmate leaves

green bracts

Hot-rock Penstemon
Penstemon deustus
Plantaginaceae

top petals withered and dried

purple lines

toothed leaves

woody stem

white-yellow flowers

Sierra Corydalis
Corydalis caseana
Papaveraceae

pinnately compound leaves

Pilose Paintbrush
Castilleja pilosa
Orobanchaceae
high elevation, eastern Sierra

divided leaves

8

Irregular Flowers: Pea Family

Flowers in the pea family bloom first near the bottom of the cluster and then open progressively further up the inflorescence. Look for developing pea pods among dried lower flowers.

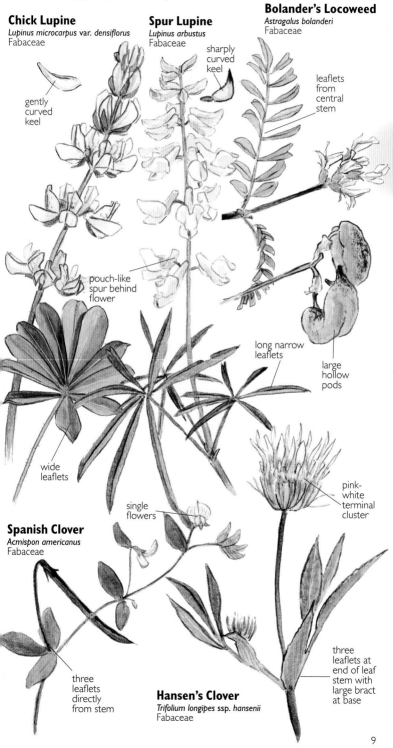

Chick Lupine
Lupinus microcarpus var. densiflorus
Fabaceae

gently curved keel

Spur Lupine
Lupinus arbustus
Fabaceae

sharply curved keel

pouch-like spur behind flower

wide leaflets

Bolander's Locoweed
Astragalus bolanderi
Fabaceae

leaflets from central stem

long narrow leaflets

large hollow pods

pink-white terminal cluster

single flowers

Spanish Clover
Acmispon americanus
Fabaceae

three leaflets directly from stem

Hansen's Clover
Trifolium longipes ssp. hansenii
Fabaceae

three leaflets at end of leaf stem with large bract at base

Small White Flowers in Clumps

Pussypaws flowers are flat on the ground in early morning but as the day and the ground heat up, the flower stems lift the blossoms away from the scorching earth.

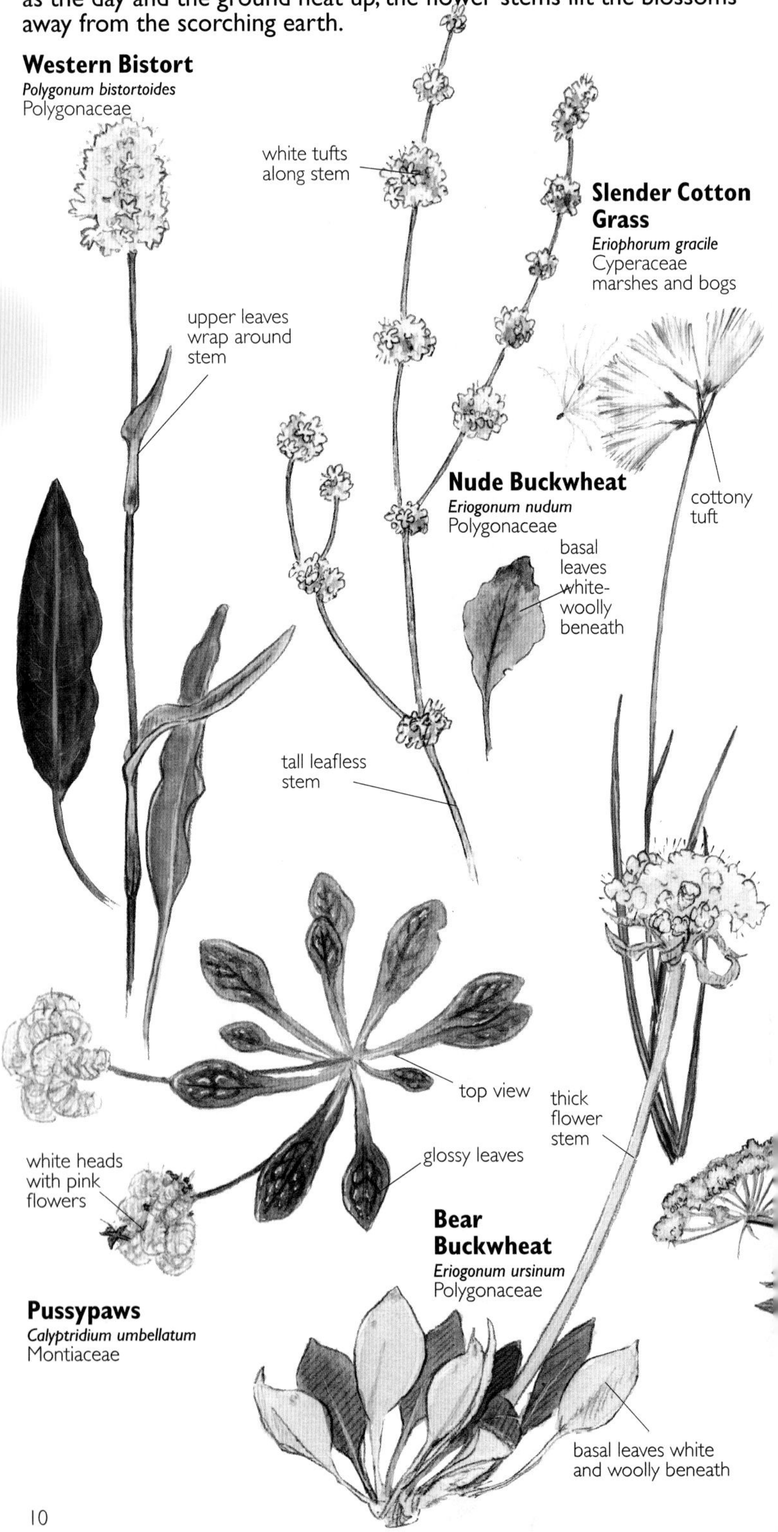

Western Bistort
Polygonum bistortoides
Polygonaceae

white tufts along stem

upper leaves wrap around stem

Slender Cotton Grass
Eriophorum gracile
Cyperaceae
marshes and bogs

cottony tuft

Nude Buckwheat
Eriogonum nudum
Polygonaceae

basal leaves white-woolly beneath

tall leafless stem

top view

thick flower stem

white heads with pink flowers

glossy leaves

Bear Buckwheat
Eriogonum ursinum
Polygonaceae

Pussypaws
Calyptridium umbellatum
Montiaceae

basal leaves white and woolly beneath

Small White Flowers in Clumps

As its name implies, Poison Hemlock contains powerful alkaloids that cause trembling, coma, and death. In 399 BC, the philosopher Socrates was poisoned with a preparation of this plant.

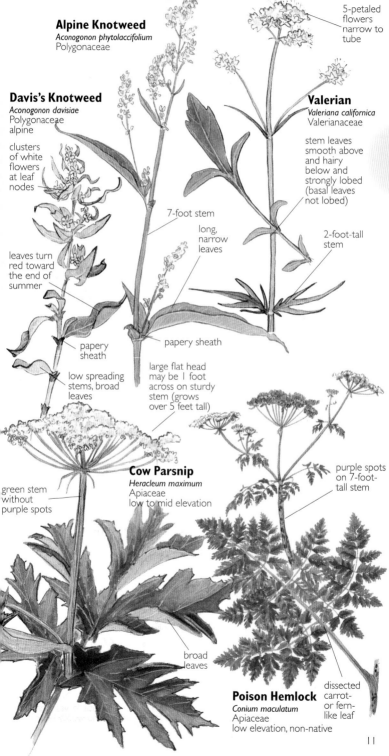

5-petaled flowers narrow to tube

Alpine Knotweed
Aconogonon phytolaccifolium
Polygonaceae

Davis's Knotweed
Aconogonon davisiae
Polygonaceae
alpine

Valerian
Valeriana californica
Valerianaceae

clusters of white flowers at leaf nodes

stem leaves smooth above and hairy below and strongly lobed (basal leaves not lobed)

7-foot stem

long, narrow leaves

2-foot-tall stem

leaves turn red toward the end of summer

papery sheath

papery sheath

low spreading stems, broad leaves

large flat head may be 1 foot across on sturdy stem (grows over 5 feet tall)

Cow Parsnip
Heracleum maximum
Apiaceae
low to mid elevation

purple spots on 7-foot-tall stem

green stem without purple spots

broad leaves

dissected carrot- or fern-like leaf

Poison Hemlock
Conium maculatum
Apiaceae
low elevation, non-native

11

Small White Flowers Forming an Umbrella (Umbel)

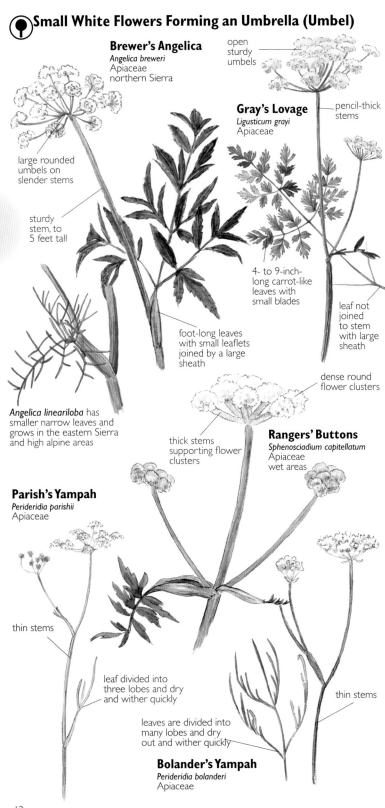

Brewer's Angelica
Angelica breweri
Apiaceae
northern Sierra

large rounded umbels on slender stems

sturdy stem, to 5 feet tall

open sturdy umbels

Gray's Lovage
Ligusticum grayi
Apiaceae

pencil-thick stems

4- to 9-inch-long carrot-like leaves with small blades

leaf not joined to stem with large sheath

foot-long leaves with small leaflets joined by a large sheath

Angelica lineariloba has smaller narrow leaves and grows in the eastern Sierra and high alpine areas

dense round flower clusters

thick stems supporting flower clusters

Rangers' Buttons
Sphenosciadium capitellatum
Apiaceae
wet areas

Parish's Yampah
Perideridia parishii
Apiaceae

thin stems

leaf divided into three lobes and dry and wither quickly

leaves are divided into many lobes and dry out and wither quickly

thin stems

Bolander's Yampah
Perideridia bolanderi
Apiaceae

12

Ancient Greek Medicine

The legendary Achilles is said to have learned the healing powers of yarrow (*Achillea*) from the Centaurs. It contains a mild anticoagulant.

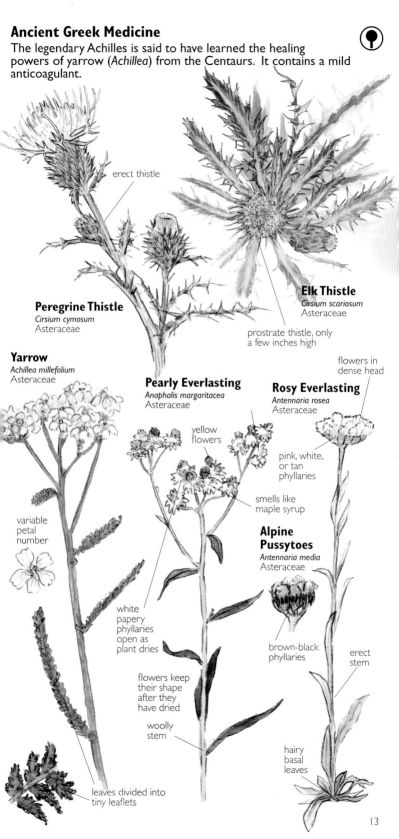

erect thistle

Peregrine Thistle
Cirsium cymosum
Asteraceae

Elk Thistle
Cirsium scariosum
Asteraceae

prostrate thistle, only a few inches high

Yarrow
Achillea millefolium
Asteraceae

Pearly Everlasting
Anaphalis margaritacea
Asteraceae

yellow flowers

Rosy Everlasting
Antennaria rosea
Asteraceae

flowers in dense head

pink, white, or tan phyllaries

smells like maple syrup

variable petal number

Alpine Pussytoes
Antennaria media
Asteraceae

white papery phyllaries open as plant dries

brown-black phyllaries

erect stem

flowers keep their shape after they have dried

woolly stem

hairy basal leaves

leaves divided into tiny leaflets

13

Biological Warfare

Knapweed is a non-native invasive plant that uses plant poisons to out-compete neighboring plants of other species.

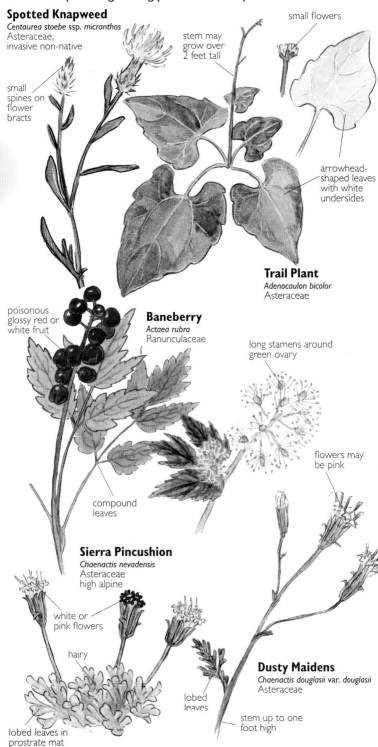

Spotted Knapweed
Centaurea stoebe ssp. *micranthos*
Asteraceae,
invasive non-native

small flowers

stem may grow over 2 feet tall

small spines on flower bracts

arrowhead-shaped leaves with white undersides

Trail Plant
Adenocaulon bicolor
Asteraceae

poisonous glossy red or white fruit

Baneberry
Actaea rubra
Ranunculaceae

long stamens around green ovary

flowers may be pink

compound leaves

Sierra Pincushion
Chaenactis nevadensis
Asteraceae
high alpine

white or pink flowers

hairy

Dusty Maidens
Chaenactis douglasii var. *douglasii*
Asteraceae

lobed leaves

stem up to one foot high

lobed leaves in prostrate mat

14

Beautiful Grass

Calochortus, in Greek, means "beautiful grass," a fitting name for these plants. Note that the leaves have parallel veins like grass blades.

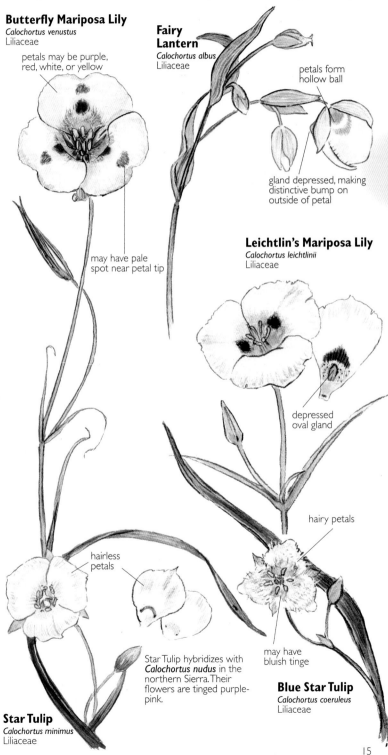

Butterfly Mariposa Lily
Calochortus venustus
Liliaceae

petals may be purple, red, white, or yellow

may have pale spot near petal tip

Fairy Lantern
Calochortus albus
Liliaceae

petals form hollow ball

gland depressed, making distinctive bump on outside of petal

Leichtlin's Mariposa Lily
Calochortus leichtlinii
Liliaceae

depressed oval gland

hairless petals

hairy petals

may have bluish tinge

Star Tulip hybridizes with **Calochortus nudus** in the northern Sierra. Their flowers are tinged purple-pink.

Blue Star Tulip
Calochortus coeruleus
Liliaceae

Star Tulip
Calochortus minimus
Liliaceae

15

③ ④ Flowers under a Magnifying Glass

Look at flowers carefully with magnification. If you do not have a hand lens, turn your binoculars upside down and hold them to one eye as you bring the subject very close to the eyepiece.

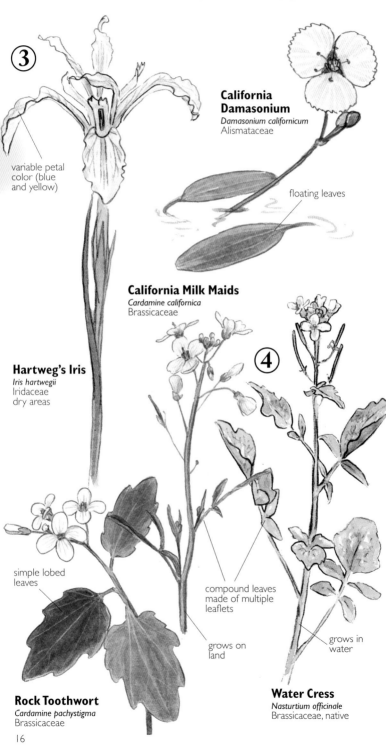

③

variable petal color (blue and yellow)

California Damasonium
Damasonium californicum
Alismataceae

floating leaves

California Milk Maids
Cardamine californica
Brassicaceae

Hartweg's Iris
Iris hartwegii
Iridaceae
dry areas

④

simple lobed leaves

compound leaves made of multiple leaflets

grows on land

grows in water

Rock Toothwort
Cardamine pachystigma
Brassicaceae

Water Cress
Nasturtium officinale
Brassicaceae, native

Lethal Genes

Groundsmoke genetics are beautifully complex and incorporate such bizarre systems as sets of chromosomes that kill half of its own pollen grains and ovules, and tetraploid hybrid species with four sets of chromosomes instead of two.

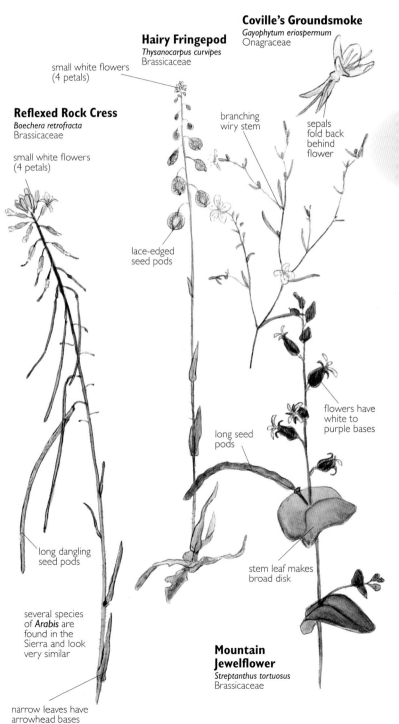

Coville's Groundsmoke
Gayophytum eriospermum
Onagraceae

Hairy Fringepod
Thysanocarpus curvipes
Brassicaceae

small white flowers
(4 petals)

branching
wiry stem

sepals
fold back
behind
flower

Reflexed Rock Cress
Boechera retrofracta
Brassicaceae

small white flowers
(4 petals)

lace-edged
seed pods

flowers have
white to
purple bases

long seed
pods

long dangling
seed pods

stem leaf makes
broad disk

several species
of **Arabis** are
found in the
Sierra and look
very similar

Mountain Jewelflower
Streptanthus tortuosus
Brassicaceae

narrow leaves have
arrowhead bases

⑤ Hawkmoth Pollination

Alpine Columbine is pollinated by hawkmoths, which are attracted to white upright flowers. Compare this species with the hummingbird-pollinated Red Columbine.

flowers point up, may have pink tinge

Alpine Columbine
Aquilegia pubescens
Ranunculaceae

long nectar tubes

basal leaves

Waterfall Buttercup
Ranunculus hystriculus
Ranunculaceae
near water

flowers may have pink tinge

Richardson's Geranium
Geranium richardsonii
Geraniaceae

Indian Rhubarb
Darmera peltata
Saxifragaceae

long seed pods

leaves one foot wide

grows at stream edge

18

Tube- or Cone-shaped Flowers

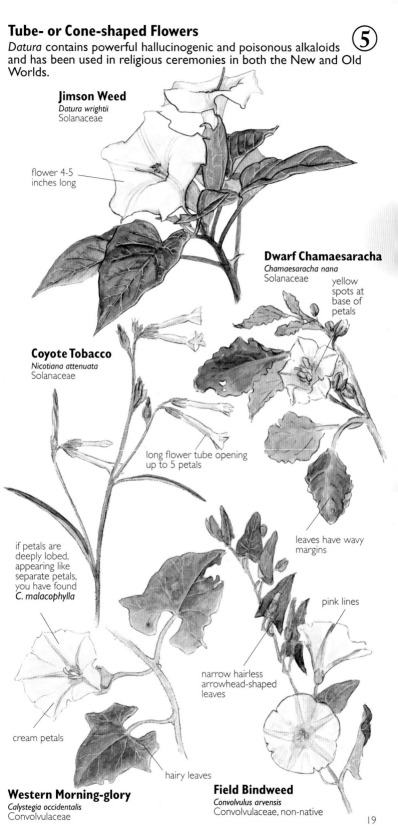

Datura contains powerful hallucinogenic and poisonous alkaloids and has been used in religious ceremonies in both the New and Old Worlds.

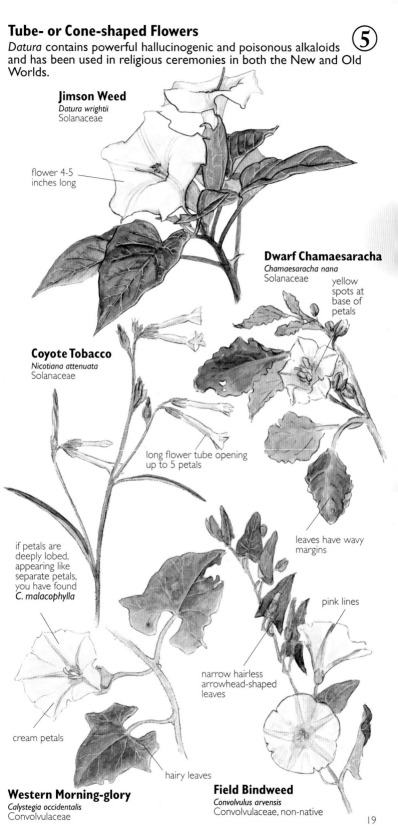

Jimson Weed
Datura wrightii
Solanaceae

flower 4-5 inches long

Dwarf Chamaesaracha
Chamaesaracha nana
Solanaceae

yellow spots at base of petals

Coyote Tobacco
Nicotiana attenuata
Solanaceae

long flower tube opening up to 5 petals

if petals are deeply lobed, appearing like separate petals, you have found *C. malacophylla*

leaves have wavy margins

pink lines

narrow hairless arrowhead-shaped leaves

cream petals

hairy leaves

Western Morning-glory
Calystegia occidentalis
Convolvulaceae

Field Bindweed
Convolvulus arvensis
Convolvulaceae, non-native

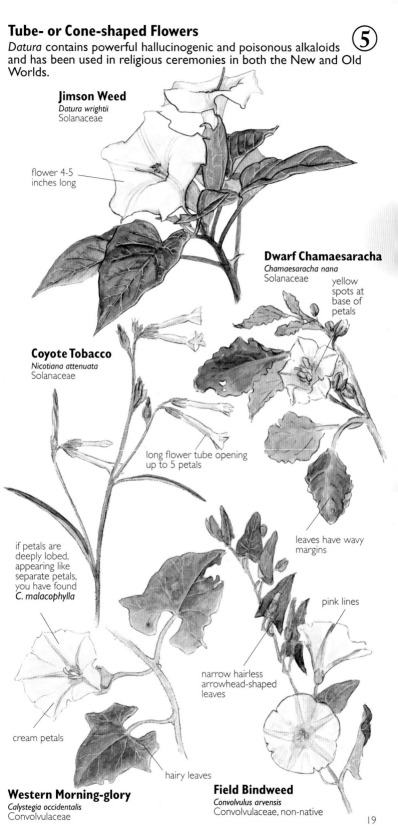

(5) Nectar Guides

To help pollinators find nectar and more efficiently pollinate a flower, many blossoms have fine lines, or nectar guides, that lead a pollinator deeper into the flower.

Western Spring Beauty

Claytonia lanceolata
Montiaceae

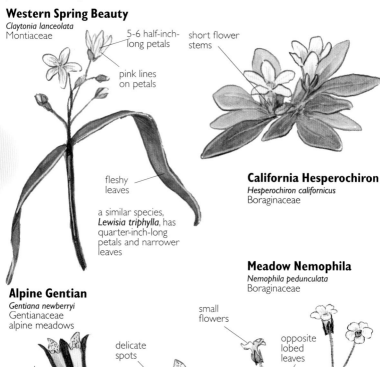

5-6 half-inch-long petals

short flower stems

pink lines on petals

fleshy leaves

a similar species, *Lewisia triphylla*, has quarter-inch-long petals and narrower leaves

California Hesperochiron

Hesperochiron californicus
Boraginaceae

Alpine Gentian

Gentiana newberryi
Gentianaceae
alpine meadows

Meadow Nemophila

Nemophila pedunculata
Boraginaceae

small flowers

delicate spots

purple-edged tubes

opposite lobed leaves

if upper leaves are alternate, you have found *N. heterophylla*

opposite basal leaves

blue lines on petal

blue spots at edge of petal

Baby Blue-eyes

Nemophila menziesii
Boraginaceae

flowers most often pale blue

opposite lobed leaves

Fivespot

Nemophila maculata
Boraginaceae

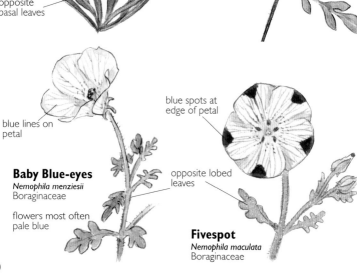

Opposite Leaves

Timing is everything. *Silene* blossoms open early in the day and wilt by the afternoon. Look for them in the morning to appreciate their beauty.

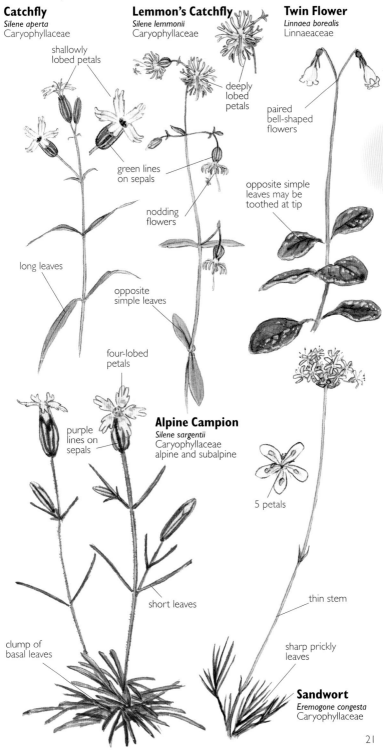

Catchfly
Silene aperta
Caryophyllaceae

shallowly lobed petals

long leaves

Lemmon's Catchfly
Silene lemmonii
Caryophyllaceae

deeply lobed petals

green lines on sepals

nodding flowers

opposite simple leaves

Twin Flower
Linnaea borealis
Linnaeaceae

paired bell-shaped flowers

opposite simple leaves may be toothed at tip

four-lobed petals

purple lines on sepals

Alpine Campion
Silene sargentii
Caryophyllaceae
alpine and subalpine

short leaves

clump of basal leaves

5 petals

thin stem

sharp prickly leaves

Sandwort
Eremogone congesta
Caryophyllaceae

⑤ Flower Perfume

Many white flowers are pollinated by moths at night. These flowers often have strong fragrances to help moths find them in the dark.

Phlox
Polemoniaceae
Three similar Phlox can be found in the Sierra. Granite Gilia looks similar but has sharp spines on the leaves.

blossom over one inch wide opens in evening

whorled leaves

Spreading Phlox
Phlox diffusa
flowers turn pink and purple after pollination, leaves not sticky

Cushion Phlox
Phlox pulvinata
sticky leaves make dense cushion, eastern Sierra

Clustered Phlox
Phlox condensata
sticky dense leaves do not make a cushion; common in alpine zone

phlox flowers can roll and appear narrower

Evening Snow
Linanthus dichotomus
Polemoniaceae

yellow tube, white petals

flower bud twists

branching, not forming mats

leaves divided into sharp spine-tipped lobes

Nuttall's Linanthus
Leptosiphon nuttallii
Polemoniaceae
often in association with sagebrush

whorled leaves

Granite Gilia
Linanthus pungens
Polemoniaceae

Sticky Traps

5

Sundew leaves are covered with sticky droplets on long red hairs. These droplets trap and digest insects. This provides the plants with essential nutrients missing in the bogs where they grow.

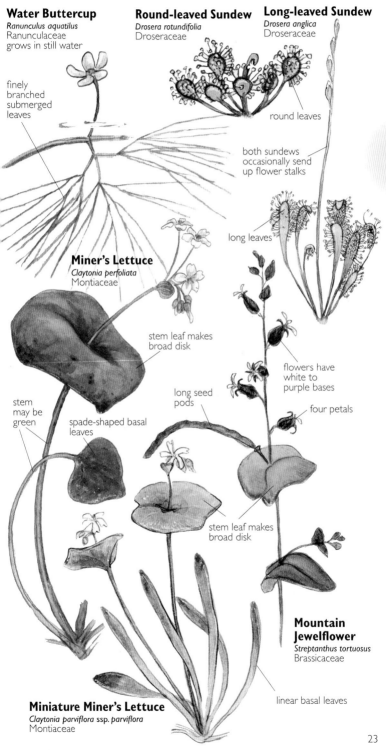

Water Buttercup
Ranunculus aquatilus
Ranunculaceae
grows in still water

finely branched submerged leaves

Round-leaved Sundew
Drosera rotundifolia
Droseraceae

Long-leaved Sundew
Drosera anglica
Droseraceae

round leaves

both sundews occasionally send up flower stalks

long leaves

Miner's Lettuce
Claytonia perfoliata
Montiaceae

stem leaf makes broad disk

stem may be green

spade-shaped basal leaves

long seed pods

flowers have white to purple bases

four petals

stem leaf makes broad disk

Mountain Jewelflower
Streptanthus tortuosus
Brassicaceae

linear basal leaves

Miniature Miner's Lettuce
Claytonia parviflora ssp. *parviflora*
Montiaceae

23

⑤ Flower Ovaries

The large structure at the very center of a flower is the ovary. Once pollinated, it produces seeds.

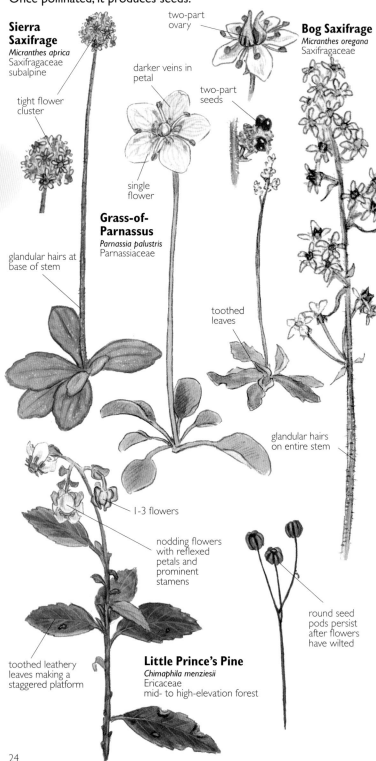

Sierra Saxifrage
Micranthes aprica
Saxifragaceae
subalpine

tight flower cluster

glandular hairs at base of stem

two-part ovary

darker veins in petal

single flower

Grass-of-Parnassus
Parnassia palustris
Parnassiaceae

two-part seeds

Bog Saxifrage
Micranthes oregana
Saxifragaceae

toothed leaves

glandular hairs on entire stem

1-3 flowers

nodding flowers with reflexed petals and prominent stamens

toothed leathery leaves making a staggered platform

round seed pods persist after flowers have wilted

Little Prince's Pine
Chimaphila menziesii
Ericaceae
mid- to high-elevation forest

Turn Over a New Leaf

⑤

The top of a leaf is dense with green chloroplasts that enable photosynthesis. The underside of a leaf has more support cells and so is often a lighter shade of green.

Small-flowered Alumroot
Heuchera micrantha
Saxifragaceae
wet areas

Pink Alumroot
Heuchera rubescens
Saxifragaceae
dry areas

base of flower pink

base of flower white or pink

flower spike often one-sided

flowers all around

toothed, lobed basal leaves

toothed basal leaves, weakly lobed

Boykinia
Boykinia major
Saxifragaceae
near streams

toothed, 8-inch basal leaves, strongly lobed

lobed petals

deeply lobed petals

flowers may be slightly toothed

basal leaf not deeply lobed

lobed basal leaf

deeply lobed leaf

Bolander's Woodland Star
Lithophragma bolanderi
Saxifragaceae
shaded damp areas

Woodland Star
Lithophragma heterophyllum
Saxifragaceae
shaded damp areas

Prairie Star
Lithophragma parviflorum
Saxifragaceae
open areas
flowers white to pink

25

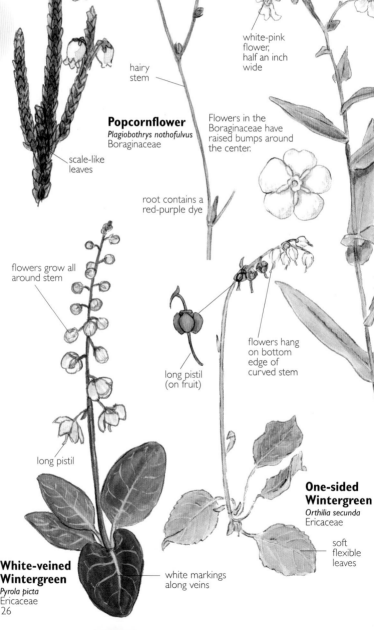

⑤ A Wildflower Loved by John Muir

"Here too... I met Cassiope growing in fringes among the battered rocks. No evangel among all the mountain plants speaks Nature's love more plainly than Cassiope."

White Heather
Cassiope mertensiana
Ericaceae

bell-shaped flower

scale-like leaves

small flowers in curled heads often with yellow centers

hairy stem

Popcornflower
Plagiobothrys nothofulvus
Boraginaceae

root contains a red-purple dye

White Stickseed
Hackelia californica
Boraginaceae

white-pink flower, half an inch wide

Flowers in the Boraginaceae have raised bumps around the center.

flowers grow all around stem

long pistil

long pistil (on fruit)

flowers hang on bottom edge of curved stem

One-sided Wintergreen
Orthilia secunda
Ericaceae

soft flexible leaves

White-veined Wintergreen
Pyrola picta
Ericaceae

white markings along veins

26

Plant and Fungus Parasites

Dodder feeds directly from the tissues of other plants. The other plants on this page parasitize fungi in the soil that may in turn have a parasitic or even beneficial relationship with the roots of nearby trees or other plants.

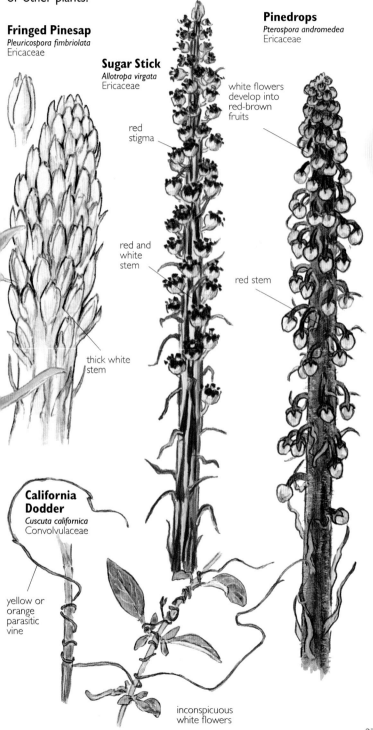

Fringed Pinesap
Pleuricospora fimbriolata
Ericaceae

Sugar Stick
Allotropa virgata
Ericaceae

Pinedrops
Pterospora andromedea
Ericaceae

white flowers develop into red-brown fruits

red stigma

red and white stem

red stem

thick white stem

California Dodder
Cuscuta californica
Convolvulaceae

yellow or orange parasitic vine

inconspicuous white flowers

27

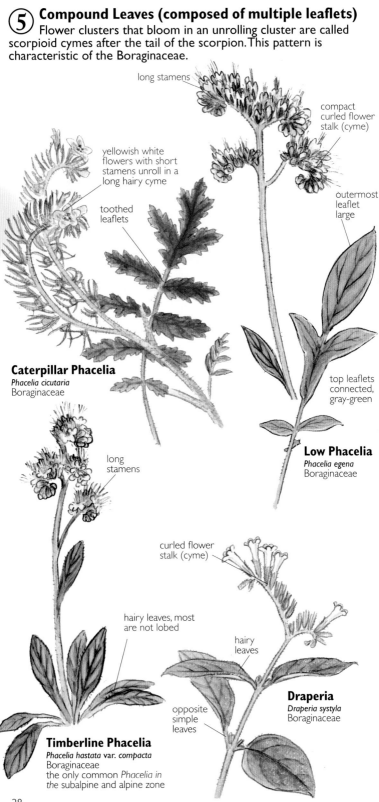

⑤ Compound Leaves (composed of multiple leaflets)

Flower clusters that bloom in an unrolling cluster are called scorpioid cymes after the tail of the scorpion. This pattern is characteristic of the Boraginaceae.

long stamens

compact curled flower stalk (cyme)

yellowish white flowers with short stamens unroll in a long hairy cyme

toothed leaflets

outermost leaflet large

Caterpillar Phacelia
Phacelia cicutaria
Boraginaceae

top leaflets connected, gray-green

Low Phacelia
Phacelia egena
Boraginaceae

long stamens

curled flower stalk (cyme)

hairy leaves, most are not lobed

hairy leaves

Draperia
Draperia systyla
Boraginaceae

opposite simple leaves

Timberline Phacelia
Phacelia hastata var. *compacta*
Boraginaceae
the only common *Phacelia* in the subalpine and alpine zone

Compound Leaves (composed of multiple leaflets)

Botanically speaking, a leaf is the entire structure that emerges above a leaf bud. It can have multiple leaf-like blades.

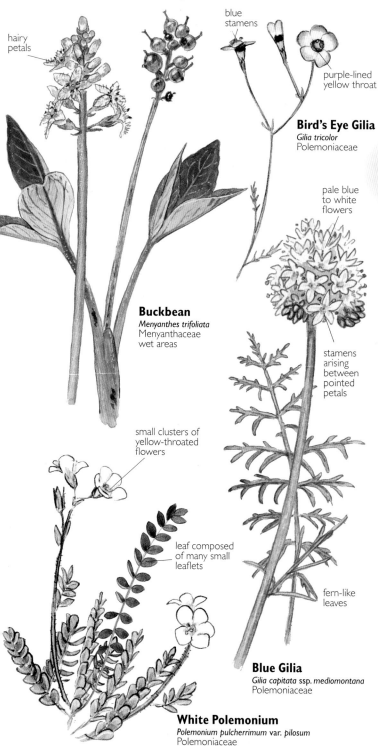

hairy petals

blue stamens

purple-lined yellow throat

Bird's Eye Gilia
Gilia tricolor
Polemoniaceae

Buckbean
Menyanthes trifoliata
Menyanthaceae
wet areas

pale blue to white flowers

stamens arising between pointed petals

small clusters of yellow-throated flowers

leaf composed of many small leaflets

fern-like leaves

Blue Gilia
Gilia capitata ssp. *mediomontana*
Polemoniaceae

White Polemonium
Polemonium pulcherrimum var. *pilosum*
Polemoniaceae

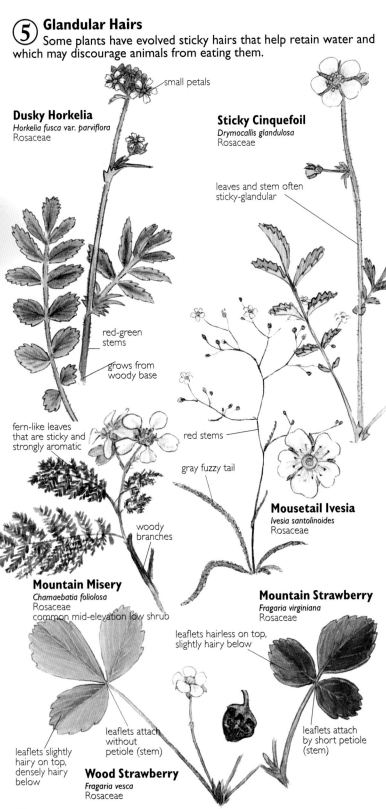

⑤ Glandular Hairs

Some plants have evolved sticky hairs that help retain water and which may discourage animals from eating them.

small petals

Dusky Horkelia
Horkelia fusca var. parviflora
Rosaceae

Sticky Cinquefoil
Drymocallis glandulosa
Rosaceae

leaves and stem often sticky-glandular

red-green stems

grows from woody base

fern-like leaves that are sticky and strongly aromatic

red stems

gray fuzzy tail

Mousetail Ivesia
Ivesia santolinoides
Rosaceae

woody branches

Mountain Misery
Chamaebatia foliolosa
Rosaceae
common mid-elevation low shrub

leaflets hairless on top, slightly hairy below

Mountain Strawberry
Fragaria virginiana
Rosaceae

leaflets attach without petiole (stem)

leaflets attach by short petiole (stem)

leaflets slightly hairy on top, densely hairy below

Wood Strawberry
Fragaria vesca
Rosaceae

A Sweet Reward

Flowers produce nectar to attract insects or birds. Once at the flower, these animals are dusted with pollen so that they may transfer this genetic material to the ovary of another plant.

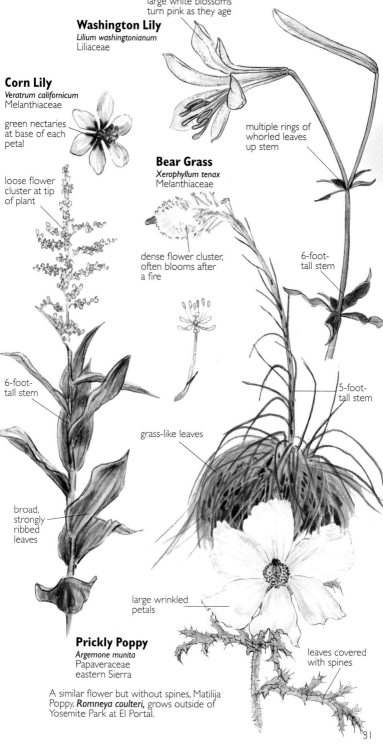

Washington Lily
Lilium washingtonianum
Liliaceae

large white blossoms turn pink as they age

Corn Lily
Veratrum californicum
Melanthiaceae

green nectaries at base of each petal

loose flower cluster at tip of plant

multiple rings of whorled leaves up stem

Bear Grass
Xerophyllum tenax
Melanthiaceae

dense flower cluster, often blooms after a fire

6-foot-tall stem

6-foot-tall stem

5-foot-tall stem

grass-like leaves

broad, strongly ribbed leaves

large wrinkled petals

Prickly Poppy
Argemone munita
Papaveraceae
eastern Sierra

leaves covered with spines

A similar flower but without spines, Matilija Poppy, *Romneya coulteri,* grows outside of Yosemite Park at El Portal.

⑥ Bulbs in a Short Growing Season

Species that grow from bulbs store sugar over a series of summers until they have enough energy to send up a flower.

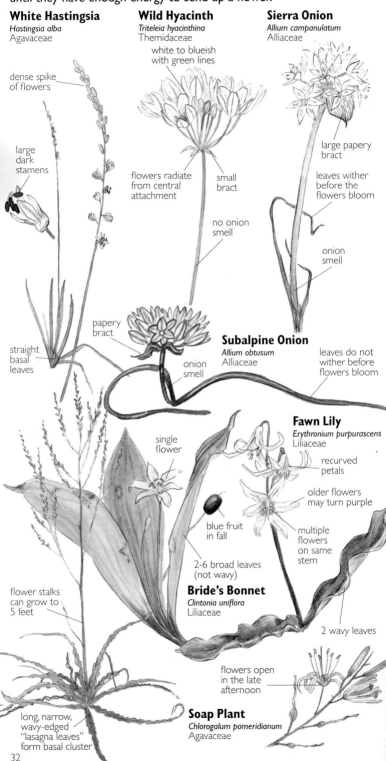

White Hastingsia
Hastingsia alba
Agavaceae

dense spike of flowers

large dark stamens

straight basal leaves

Wild Hyacinth
Triteleia hyacinthina
Themidaceae

white to blueish with green lines

flowers radiate from central attachment

small bract

no onion smell

papery bract

onion smell

Sierra Onion
Allium campanulatum
Alliaceae

large papery bract

leaves wither before the flowers bloom

onion smell

Subalpine Onion
Allium obtusum
Alliaceae

leaves do not wither before flowers bloom

Fawn Lily
Erythronium purpurascens
Liliaceae

recurved petals

older flowers may turn purple

multiple flowers on same stem

single flower

blue fruit in fall

2-6 broad leaves (not wavy)

Bride's Bonnet
Clintonia uniflora
Liliaceae

2 wavy leaves

flower stalks can grow to 5 feet

flowers open in the late afternoon

Soap Plant
Chlorogalum pomeridianum
Agavaceae

long, narrow, wavy-edged "lasagna leaves" form basal cluster

Monocots vs. Dicots

Flowering plants are divided into two groups. Plants with three or six petals typically have parallel veins in their leaves and are called **Monocots**. Plants with four, five, or many petals typically have branching veins in their leaves and are called **Dicots**.

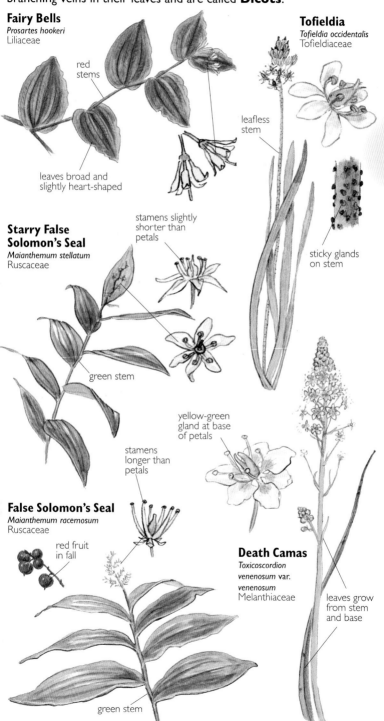

Fairy Bells
Prosartes hookeri
Liliaceae

red stems

leaves broad and slightly heart-shaped

Starry False Solomon's Seal
Maianthemum stellatum
Ruscaceae

stamens slightly shorter than petals

green stem

False Solomon's Seal
Maianthemum racemosum
Ruscaceae

red fruit in fall

stamens longer than petals

green stem

Tofieldia
Tofieldia occidentalis
Tofieldiaceae

leafless stem

sticky glands on stem

yellow-green gland at base of petals

Death Camas
Toxicoscordion venenosum var. *venenosum*
Melanthiaceae

leaves grow from stem and base

6

Lewis and Clark Species Names

(M) Bitter Root *Lewisia rediviva* was first collected in 1806 on the Lewis and Clark expedition. What other species of birds and plants can you find that bear the names of these two explorers?

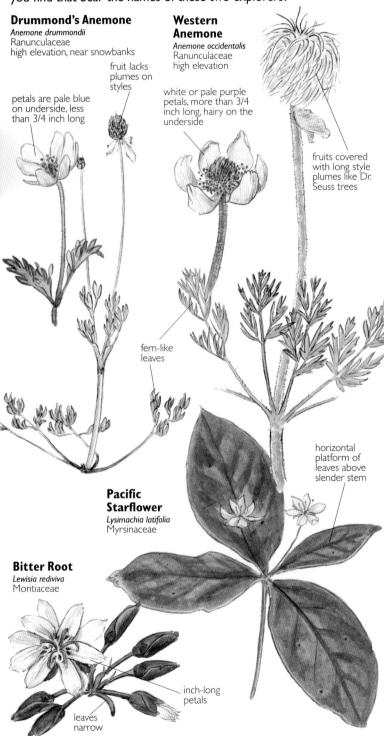

Drummond's Anemone
Anemone drummondii
Ranunculaceae
high elevation, near snowbanks

fruit lacks plumes on styles

petals are pale blue on underside, less than 3/4 inch long

Western Anemone
Anemone occidentalis
Ranunculaceae
high elevation

white or pale purple petals, more than 3/4 inch long, hairy on the underside

fruits covered with long style plumes like Dr. Seuss trees

fern-like leaves

horizontal platform of leaves above slender stem

Pacific Starflower
Lysimachia latifolia
Myrsinaceae

Bitter Root
Lewisia rediviva
Montiaceae

inch-long petals

leaves narrow

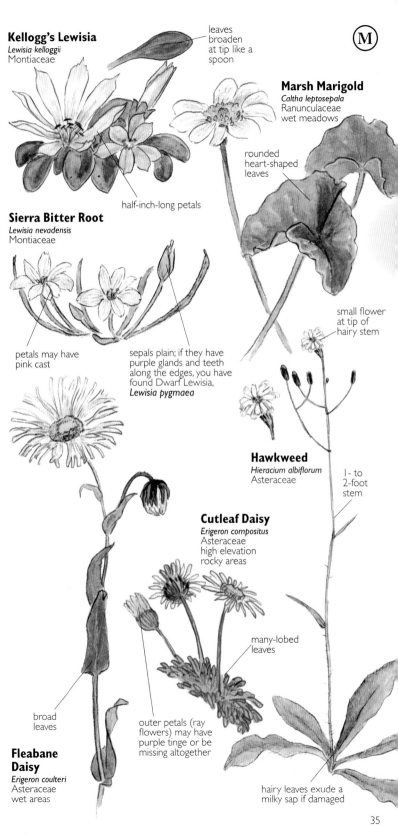

Kellogg's Lewisia
Lewisia kelloggii
Montiaceae

leaves broaden at tip like a spoon

Marsh Marigold
Caltha leptosepala
Ranunculaceae
wet meadows

rounded heart-shaped leaves

half-inch-long petals

Sierra Bitter Root
Lewisia nevadensis
Montiaceae

petals may have pink cast

sepals plain; if they have purple glands and teeth along the edges, you have found Dwarf Lewisia, *Lewisia pygmaea*

small flower at tip of hairy stem

Hawkweed
Hieracium albiflorum
Asteraceae

1- to 2-foot stem

Cutleaf Daisy
Erigeron compositus
Asteraceae
high elevation
rocky areas

many-lobed leaves

broad leaves

outer petals (ray flowers) may have purple tinge or be missing altogether

Fleabane Daisy
Erigeron coulteri
Asteraceae
wet areas

hairy leaves exude a milky sap if damaged

Red-Pink Flower Key

Choose among the groups (starting with A and AA) and follow the directions. Some species may have variable numbers of petals on different flowers, so look at several plants and flowers before starting to identify a plant.

A. Bilaterally symmetrical flowers: flowers can only be divided into similar halves along one central axis.

Go to , pages 37-40.

AA. Radially symmetrical flowers: flowers can be divided into similar halves along more than one axis. Go to B and BB below.

B. Flowers in a dense clump, making it difficult to tell the number of petals.

Go to ⬤, pages 41-42.

BB. Flowers not in a dense clump; you can count the number of petals per flower. Go to C below.

C.   3 petals, Go to **3**, page 43.

4 petals, Go to **4**, pages 43-44.

5 petals, Go to **5**, pages 45-51.

6 petals, Go to **6**, page 52.

Many petals or plants with variable numbers of petals on different flowers. This includes daisy- or sunflower-shaped plants.
Go to **M**, pages 52-53.

Monkeyflower Pollination Strategies

Lightly touch the tip of a Monkeyflower stigma and its two lips will slowly close. This traps the pollen that has been brought to the flower by an insect and prevents self-pollination as the pollinator leaves the flower.

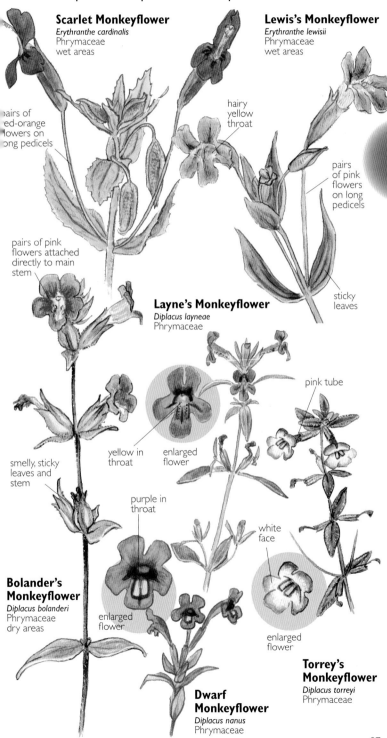

Scarlet Monkeyflower
Erythranthe cardinalis
Phrymaceae
wet areas

Lewis's Monkeyflower
Erythranthe lewisii
Phrymaceae
wet areas

pairs of red-orange flowers on long pedicels

hairy yellow throat

pairs of pink flowers on long pedicels

pairs of pink flowers attached directly to main stem

Layne's Monkeyflower
Diplacus layneae
Phrymaceae

sticky leaves

yellow in throat

enlarged flower

pink tube

smelly, sticky leaves and stem

purple in throat

white face

Bolander's Monkeyflower
Diplacus bolanderi
Phrymaceae
dry areas

enlarged flower

enlarged flower

enlarged flower

Torrey's Monkeyflower
Diplacus torreyi
Phrymaceae

Dwarf Monkeyflower
Diplacus nanus
Phrymaceae

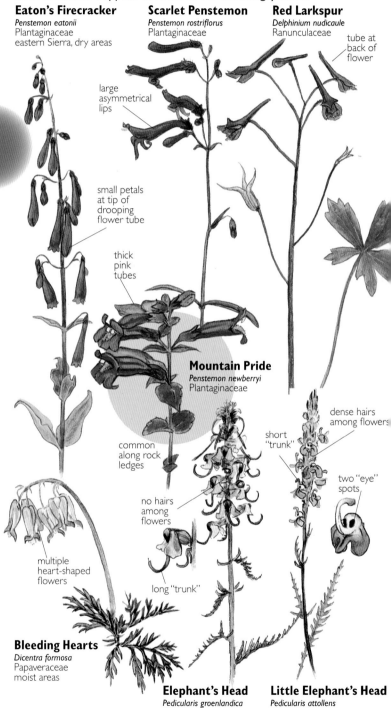

Hummingbird Flowers

Flowers that are pollinated by hummingbirds have no scent (hummingbirds can't smell), have long tubular flowers (which exclude many insects), red colors (easily seen by birds and less visible to insects) and rich nectar supplies as rewards for the hungry birds.

Eaton's Firecracker
Penstemon eatonii
Plantaginaceae
eastern Sierra, dry areas

Scarlet Penstemon
Penstemon rostriflorus
Plantaginaceae

Red Larkspur
Delphinium nudicaule
Ranunculaceae

tube at back of flower

large asymmetrical lips

small petals at tip of drooping flower tube

thick pink tubes

Mountain Pride
Penstemon newberryi
Plantaginaceae

common along rock ledges

dense hairs among flowers

short "trunk"

two "eye" spots

no hairs among flowers

multiple heart-shaped flowers

long "trunk"

Bleeding Hearts
Dicentra formosa
Papaveraceae
moist areas

Elephant's Head
Pedicularis groenlandica
Orobanchaceae
wet areas

Little Elephant's Head
Pedicularis attollens
Orobanchaceae
wet areas

Paintbrush and Owl's Clover

Paintbrush petals fuse into white or yellow tubes that extend from bright clusters of red bracts and sepals. The shapes of these petal tubes and the plant's habitat will help you identify species of paintbrush.

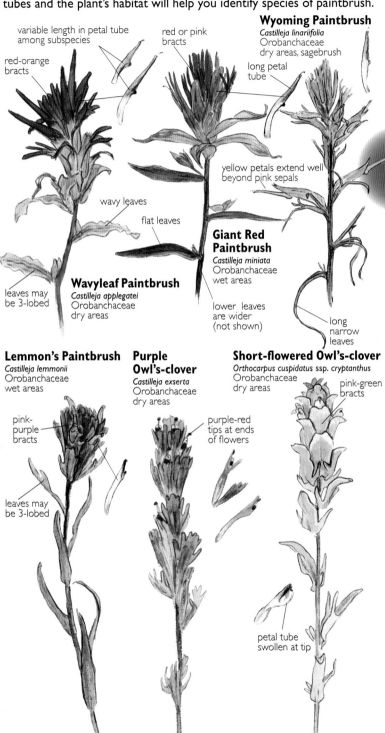

variable length in petal tube among subspecies

red or pink bracts

red-orange bracts

Wyoming Paintbrush
Castilleja linariifolia
Orobanchaceae
dry areas, sagebrush

long petal tube

yellow petals extend well beyond pink sepals

wavy leaves

flat leaves

Giant Red Paintbrush
Castilleja miniata
Orobanchaceae
wet areas

Wavyleaf Paintbrush
Castilleja applegatei
Orobanchaceae
dry areas

leaves may be 3-lobed

lower leaves are wider (not shown)

long narrow leaves

Lemmon's Paintbrush
Castilleja lemmonii
Orobanchaceae
wet areas

pink-purple bracts

leaves may be 3-lobed

Purple Owl's-clover
Castilleja exserta
Orobanchaceae
dry areas

purple-red tips at ends of flowers

Short-flowered Owl's-clover
Orthocarpus cuspidatus ssp. *cryptanthus*
Orobanchaceae
dry areas

pink-green bracts

petal tube swollen at tip

39

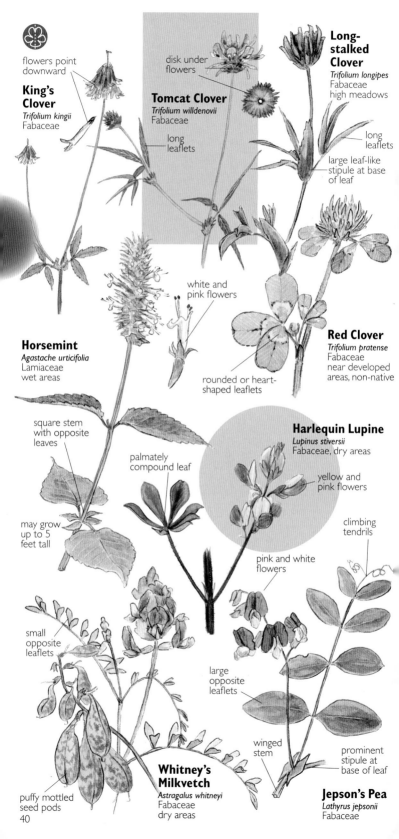

King's Clover
Trifolium kingii
Fabaceae

flowers point downward

disk under flowers

Tomcat Clover
Trifolium willdenovii
Fabaceae

long leaflets

Long-stalked Clover
Trifolium longipes
Fabaceae
high meadows

long leaflets

large leaf-like stipule at base of leaf

white and pink flowers

Horsemint
Agastache urticifolia
Lamiaceae
wet areas

square stem with opposite leaves

may grow up to 5 feet tall

rounded or heart-shaped leaflets

Red Clover
Trifolium pratense
Fabaceae
near developed areas, non-native

palmately compound leaf

Harlequin Lupine
Lupinus stiversii
Fabaceae, dry areas

yellow and pink flowers

pink and white flowers

climbing tendrils

small opposite leaflets

large opposite leaflets

winged stem

Whitney's Milkvetch
Astragalus whitneyi
Fabaceae
dry areas

puffy mottled seed pods

prominent stipule at base of leaf

Jepson's Pea
Lathyrus jepsonii
Fabaceae

40

Red Flowers with Dense Heads

Many drought-adapted plants are covered with fine white hairs. These hairs reduce water loss by reflecting sunlight and slowing air movement across the plant's surface that might whisk away moisture. Rub lightly on a patch of hairs to reveal the green chlorophyll-rich tissues beneath.

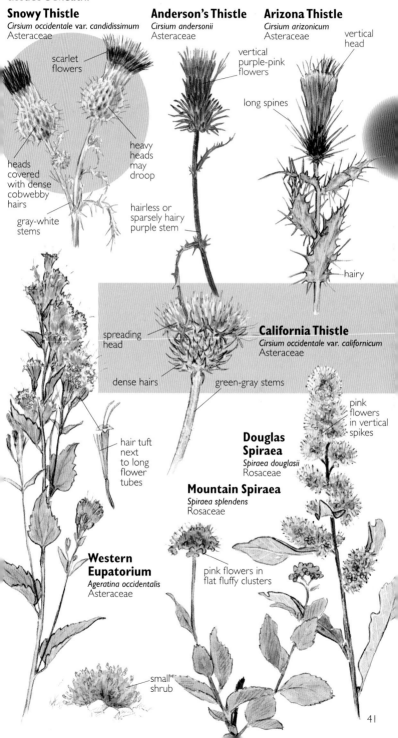

Snowy Thistle
Cirsium occidentale var. *candidissimum*
Asteraceae

scarlet flowers

heads covered with dense cobwebby hairs

gray-white stems

Anderson's Thistle
Cirsium andersonii
Asteraceae

vertical purple-pink flowers

heavy heads may droop

hairless or sparsely hairy purple stem

Arizona Thistle
Cirsium arizonicum
Asteraceae

vertical head

long spines

hairy

spreading head

California Thistle
Cirsium occidentale var. *californicum*
Asteraceae

dense hairs

green-gray stems

hair tuft next to long flower tubes

Western Eupatorium
Ageratina occidentalis
Asteraceae

Douglas Spiraea
Spiraea douglasii
Rosaceae

pink flowers in vertical spikes

Mountain Spiraea
Spiraea splendens
Rosaceae

pink flowers in flat fluffy clusters

small shrub

Cushion Plants

Many high-elevation plants grow from a low pad of leaves. This growth form helps them avoid the drying wind and absorb heat from the sun-warmed ground.

Pussypaws

Calyptridium monospermum
Montiaceae

pink flowers

spoon-shaped leaves in basal rosette

top view

Prostrate or Lobb's Buckwheat

Eriogonum lobbii
Polygonaceae

flower stems sprawl on ground

leaf-like bracts

large woolly leaves

open flower cluster

Mountain Sorrel

Oxyria digyna
Polygonaceae

long branching stems

red-purple seed pod

Wright's Buckwheat

Eriogonum wrightii
Polygonaceae

Rosewort

Rhodiola integrifolia
Crassulaceae
wet areas

short stem

thick leaves

often grows in wet moss

round or heart-shaped leaves

Sierra Chaenactis

Chaenactis nevadensis
Asteraceae
dry areas, high elevation

protective bracts

Oval-leaved Buckwheat

Eriogonum ovalifolium
Polygonaceae
alpine ridges

variable flower color

small round leaves in compact cushion

lobed leaf

42

After the Burn

Fire-adapted species such as Fireweed thrive in the nutrient-rich soils that develop after a burn.

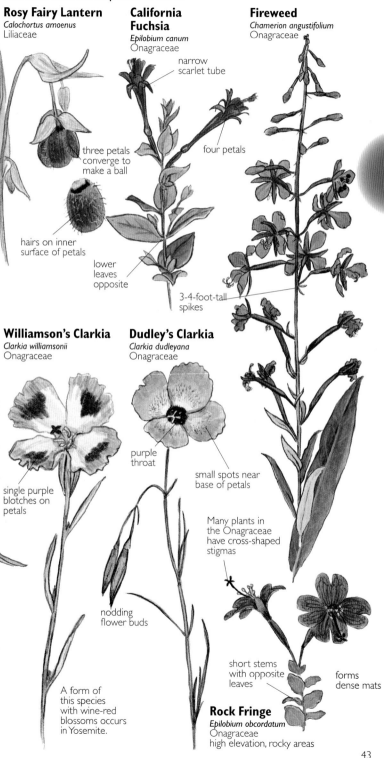

Rosy Fairy Lantern
Calochortus amoenus
Liliaceae

three petals converge to make a ball

hairs on inner surface of petals

California Fuchsia
Epilobium canum
Onagraceae

narrow scarlet tube

four petals

lower leaves opposite

Fireweed
Chamerion angustifolium
Onagraceae

3-4-foot-tall spikes

Williamson's Clarkia
Clarkia williamsonii
Onagraceae

single purple blotches on petals

A form of this species with wine-red blossoms occurs in Yosemite.

Dudley's Clarkia
Clarkia dudleyana
Onagraceae

purple throat

small spots near base of petals

Many plants in the Onagraceae have cross-shaped stigmas

nodding flower buds

short stems with opposite leaves

forms dense mats

Rock Fringe
Epilobium obcordatum
Onagraceae
high elevation, rocky areas

43

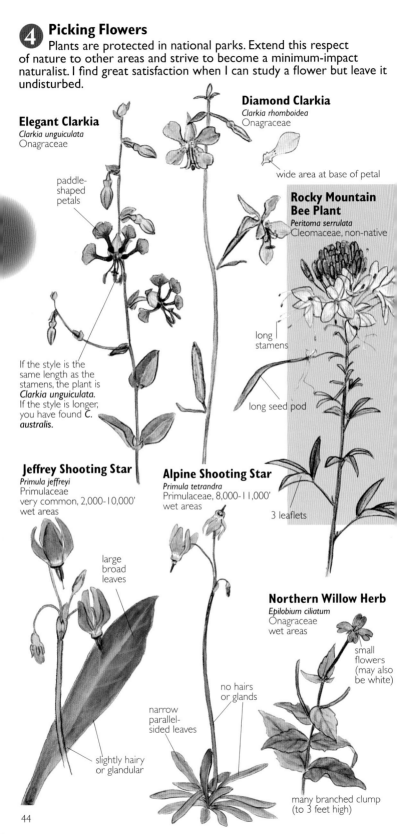

4 Picking Flowers

Plants are protected in national parks. Extend this respect of nature to other areas and strive to become a minimum-impact naturalist. I find great satisfaction when I can study a flower but leave it undisturbed.

Elegant Clarkia
Clarkia unguiculata
Onagraceae

paddle-shaped petals

If the style is the same length as the stamens, the plant is *Clarkia unguiculata*. If the style is longer, you have found *C. australis*.

Diamond Clarkia
Clarkia rhomboidea
Onagraceae

wide area at base of petal

Rocky Mountain Bee Plant
Peritoma serrulata
Cleomaceae, non-native

long stamens

long seed pod

3 leaflets

Jeffrey Shooting Star
Primula jeffreyi
Primulaceae
very common, 2,000-10,000'
wet areas

large broad leaves

slightly hairy or glandular

Alpine Shooting Star
Primula tetrandra
Primulaceae, 8,000-11,000'
wet areas

no hairs or glands

narrow parallel-sided leaves

Northern Willow Herb
Epilobium ciliatum
Onagraceae
wet areas

small flowers (may also be white)

many branched clump (to 3 feet high)

Shooting Star Pollination

Shooting Stars are "buzz pollinated." Bees grab the anthers and vibrate their wing muscles at a frequency that shakes the pollen loose. Listen carefully to these pollinating bees. You can hear the change in frequency!

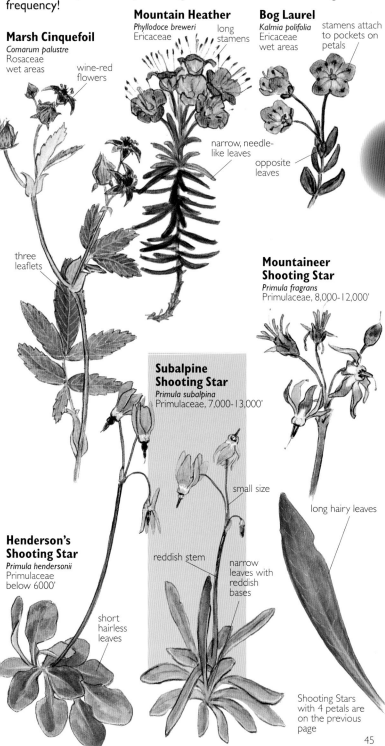

Mountain Heather
Phyllodoce breweri
Ericaceae

long stamens

Bog Laurel
Kalmia polifolia
Ericaceae
wet areas

stamens attach to pockets on petals

Marsh Cinquefoil
Comarum palustre
Rosaceae
wet areas

wine-red flowers

narrow, needle-like leaves

opposite leaves

three leaflets

Mountaineer Shooting Star
Primula fragrans
Primulaceae, 8,000-12,000'

Subalpine Shooting Star
Primula subalpina
Primulaceae, 7,000-13,000'

small size

long hairy leaves

Henderson's Shooting Star
Primula hendersonii
Primulaceae
below 6000'

reddish stem

narrow leaves with reddish bases

short hairless leaves

Shooting Stars with 4 petals are on the previous page

45

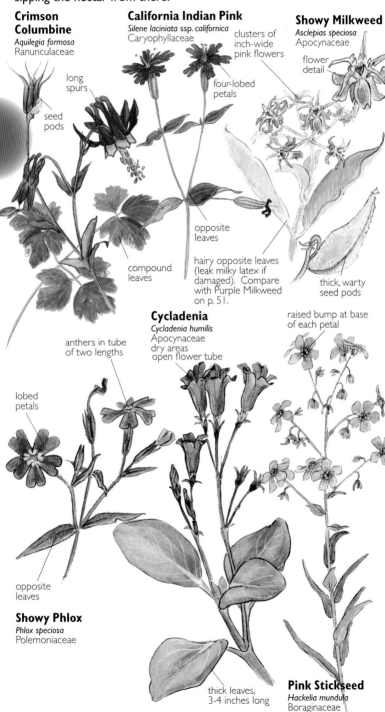

5 Nectar Thieves

Columbine flowers produce large amounts of nectar at the ends of their spurs to attract hummingbirds. A constriction at the end of the spur prevents bees from crawling down into it. Some bees get around this defense by cutting a hole at the base of the tube and sipping the nectar from there.

Crimson Columbine

Aquilegia formosa
Ranunculaceae

long spurs

seed pods

compound leaves

California Indian Pink

Silene laciniata ssp. *californica*
Caryophyllaceae

clusters of inch-wide pink flowers

four-lobed petals

opposite leaves

hairy opposite leaves (leak milky latex if damaged). Compare with Purple Milkweed on p. 51.

Showy Milkweed

Asclepias speciosa
Apocynaceae

flower detail

thick, warty seed pods

Cycladenia

Cycladenia humilis
Apocynaceae
dry areas
open flower tube

raised bump at base of each petal

anthers in tube of two lengths

lobed petals

opposite leaves

Showy Phlox

Phlox speciosa
Polemoniaceae

thick leaves, 3-4 inches long

Pink Stickseed

Hackelia mundula
Boraginaceae

Color Change and Pollination

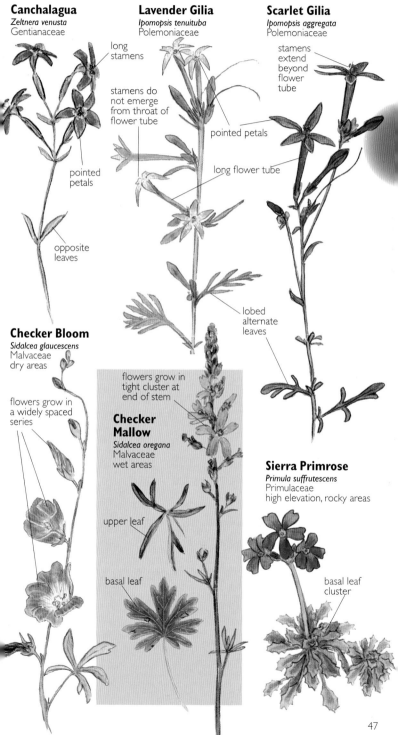

Early in the season, you will find bright red Scarlet Gilia blossoms. Late-season flowers may be pink or pinkish-white. The early flowers attract hummingbirds while the late flowers are more easily seen by long-tongued sphinx moths that fly at dusk.

Canchalagua
Zeltnera venusta
Gentianaceae

long stamens

pointed petals

opposite leaves

Lavender Gilia
Ipomopsis tenuituba
Polemoniaceae

stamens do not emerge from throat of flower tube

pointed petals

long flower tube

lobed alternate leaves

Scarlet Gilia
Ipomopsis aggregata
Polemoniaceae

stamens extend beyond flower tube

Checker Bloom
Sidalcea glaucescens
Malvaceae
dry areas

flowers grow in a widely spaced series

Checker Mallow
Sidalcea oregana
Malvaceae
wet areas

flowers grow in tight cluster at end of stem

upper leaf

basal leaf

Sierra Primrose
Primula suffrutescens
Primulaceae
high elevation, rocky areas

basal leaf cluster

⑤ Plants without Chlorophyll

Some species of plants lack the green pigment chlorophyll required to synthesize sugars (plant food) in sunlight. For many years it was believed that these plants fed upon decomposing matter in the soil as fungi do. Such plants were called Saprotrophs. Recent studies have shown that the plants do not feed upon matter in the soil but are parasites on soil fungi. These fungi may in turn be connected to the roots of green plants with which they exchange sugar, water, or nutrients. These mycotrophic (fungus eating) plants may receive sugars from the photosynthetic work of neighboring plants through a fungus bridge. While both the host green plant and the fungi benefit from their mycorrhizal (fungus-root) relationship, the odd reddish plants are freeloaders.

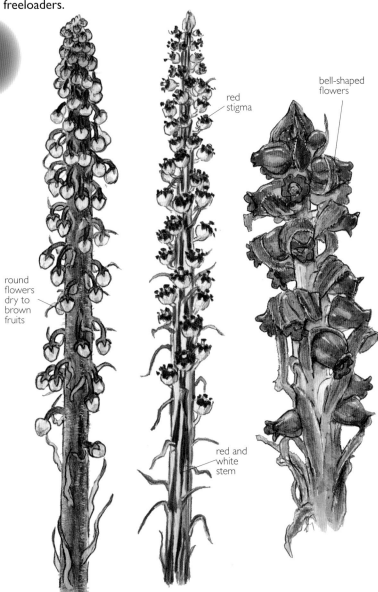

round flowers dry to brown fruits

red stigma

bell-shaped flowers

red and white stem

Pinedrops
Pterospora andromedea
Ericaceae
48

Sugar Stick
Allotropa virgata
Ericaceae

Snow Plant
Sarcodes sanguinea
Ericaceae

Orchid Seeds

Orchids are notoriously difficult to grow from seeds.
They produce millions of nearly microscopic seeds that will only germinate if they land where a symbiotic mycorrhizal fungus also lives. Without this fungus, the orchid cannot survive. Photosynthetic orchids (ones with green pigment) become less dependent on the fungus as they mature and develop leaves. Coralroot Orchids are parasites and remain dependent on their host fungus throughout their lives.

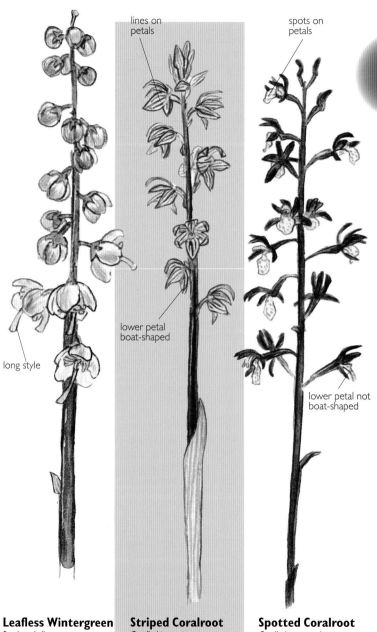

lines on petals

spots on petals

long style

lower petal boat-shaped

lower petal not boat-shaped

Leafless Wintergreen
Pyrola aphylla
Ericaceae

Striped Coralroot
Corallorhiza striata
Orchidaceae

Spotted Coralroot
Corallorhiza maculata
Orchidaceae

49

Edible and Useful

Pipsissewa is a charming wildflower that has been used medicinally to treat kidney problems and also provides part of the flavor in root beer.

Prince's Pine, Pipsissewa
Chimaphila umbellata
Ericaceae

nodding flowers with reflexed petals and prominent stamens

3-7 flowers

saw-toothed leaves in whorls

Bog Wintergreen
Pyrola asarifolia
Ericaceae
wet areas

long pistil

round leaves

Sierra Bolandra
Bolandra californica
Saxifragaceae
damp woods

narrow red petals

woolly seed head

bulbous flowers

cup-shaped flower with fringed edges

glandular-hairy

fern-like leaves

Prairie Smoke
Geum triflorum
Rosaceae

Fringe Cups
Tellima grandiflora
Saxifragaceae

Milkweed Poison and Insect Relationships

5

Milkweed sap contains heart poisons called cardenolides. These chemicals deter many animals from eating the plants. However, some insects can ingest the poisons, even storing them in their own bodies to provide some defense against predators. Look for such brightly colored insects on milkweed plants.

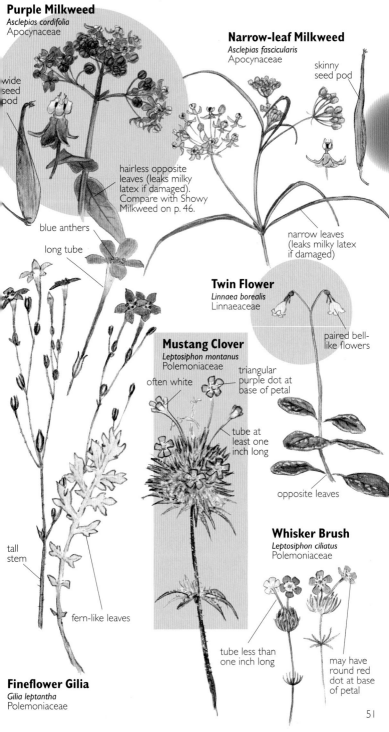

Purple Milkweed
Asclepias cordifolia
Apocynaceae

wide seed pod

blue anthers

long tube

Narrow-leaf Milkweed
Asclepias fascicularis
Apocynaceae

skinny seed pod

hairless opposite leaves (leaks milky latex if damaged). Compare with Showy Milkweed on p. 46.

narrow leaves (leaks milky latex if damaged)

Twin Flower
Linnaea borealis
Linnaeaceae

paired bell-like flowers

Mustang Clover
Leptosiphon montanus
Polemoniaceae

often white

triangular purple dot at base of petal

tube at least one inch long

opposite leaves

tall stem

fern-like leaves

Whisker Brush
Leptosiphon ciliatus
Polemoniaceae

tube less than one inch long

may have round red dot at base of petal

Fineflower Gilia
Gilia leptantha
Polemoniaceae

6 M Seed Pods

After fertilization, the ovary develops into a seed pod. Try to determine how a pod will spread its seeds: wind, being eaten by animals, hitchhiking...

Scarlet Fritillary
Fritillaria recurva
Liliaceae

six-angled
seed pod

red-
orange
bells

whorled
leaves

Bitter Root
Lewisia rediviva
Montiaceae
white or pink petals

inconspicuous leaves

succulent stem
covered with
bristly bumps

5-7 petals

Beavertail Cactus
Opuntia basilaris
Cactaceae

horizontal
platform of leaves
above slender
stem

Pacific Starflower
Lysimachia latifolia
Myrsinaceae

Plants with Variable Numbers of Petals

Some species such as Starflower and Congdon's Lewisia vary in the numbers of petals on each flower. Stephanomeria "flowers" are actually flower clusters with each apparent petal a separate flower.

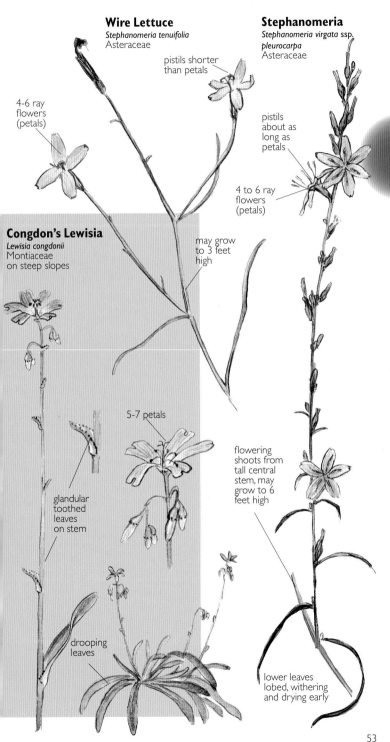

Wire Lettuce
Stephanomeria tenuifolia
Asteraceae

pistils shorter than petals

4-6 ray flowers (petals)

Stephanomeria
Stephanomeria virgata ssp. *pleurocarpa*
Asteraceae

pistils about as long as petals

4 to 6 ray flowers (petals)

Congdon's Lewisia
Lewisia congdonii
Montiaceae
on steep slopes

may grow to 3 feet high

5-7 petals

glandular toothed leaves on stem

flowering shoots from tall central stem, may grow to 6 feet high

drooping leaves

lower leaves lobed, withering and drying early

Orange Flower Key

Choose among the groups (starting with A and AA) and follow the directions. Some species may have variable numbers of petals on different flowers, so look at several plants and flowers before starting to identify a plant.

A. Bilaterally symmetrical flowers: flowers can only be divided into similar halves along one central axis.

Go to , page 55.

AA. Radially symmetrical flowers: flowers can be divided into similar halves along more than one axis. Go to B below.

B.   4 petals, Go to , page 55.

       5 petals, Go to ⑤ , page 56.

       6 petals, Go to ⑥ , page 57.

Parasitic Orange String

Chlorophyll is the primary pigment that plants use to photosynthesize, or produce sugar using sunlight energy. It is green in color. Plants that are parasitic lack this green pigment and get their energy by feeding on the tissues of other plants or fungi. Dodder wraps its orange tendrils around green plants and feeds through tiny rootlets it inserts into its host.

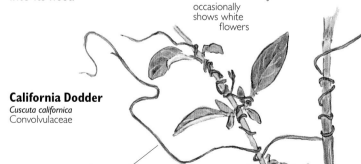

occasionally shows white flowers

California Dodder
Cuscuta californica
Convolvulaceae

may form dense orange mats

Golden Poppies?

California Poppies that grow near the coast have golden petals with orange interiors (Golden Poppies) while those found inland are orange.

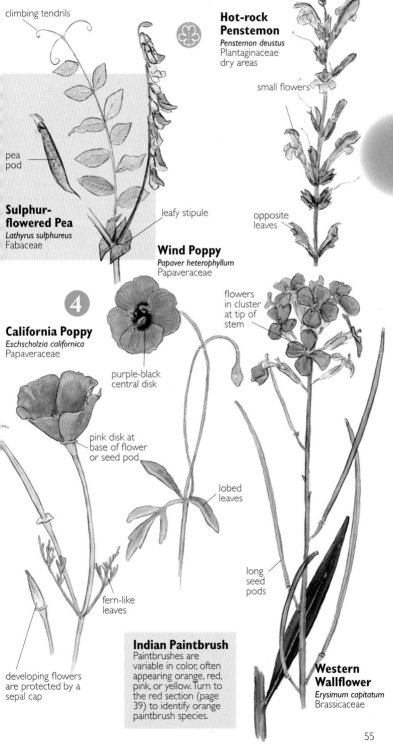

climbing tendrils

Hot-rock Penstemon
Penstemon deustus
Plantaginaceae
dry areas

small flowers

pea pod

Sulphur-flowered Pea
Lathyrus sulphureus
Fabaceae

leafy stipule

opposite leaves

Wind Poppy
Papaver heterophyllum
Papaveraceae

flowers in cluster at tip of stem

4

California Poppy
Eschscholzia californica
Papaveraceae

purple-black central disk

pink disk at base of flower or seed pod

lobed leaves

long seed pods

fern-like leaves

Indian Paintbrush
Paintbrushes are variable in color, often appearing orange, red, pink, or yellow. Turn to the red section (page 39) to identify orange paintbrush species.

developing flowers are protected by a sepal cap

Western Wallflower
Erysimum capitatum
Brassicaceae

5 Unrolling Flowers

Fiddleneck buds uncurl from a tightly coiled ball. As flowers bloom, the ball unrolls to reveal new buds, which bloom in succession. Look for similar structures in other flowers such as Phacelia and Forget-Me-Nots.

Common Fiddleneck
Amsinckia intermedia
Boraginaceae
low elevation

fiddleneck of orange flowers

Grand Collomia
Collomia grandiflora
Polemoniaceae

pale salmon-orange trumpet-shaped flowers

stamens have blue anthers

thorny shrub

Mountain Gooseberry
Ribes montigenum
Grossulariaceae

flowers ripen into red berries

Hover Pollination

6

Large lilies do not provide a landing pad for pollinators. When hummingbirds visit the flower, they hover below the drooping blossom, where they are dusted with pollen by the extended anthers.

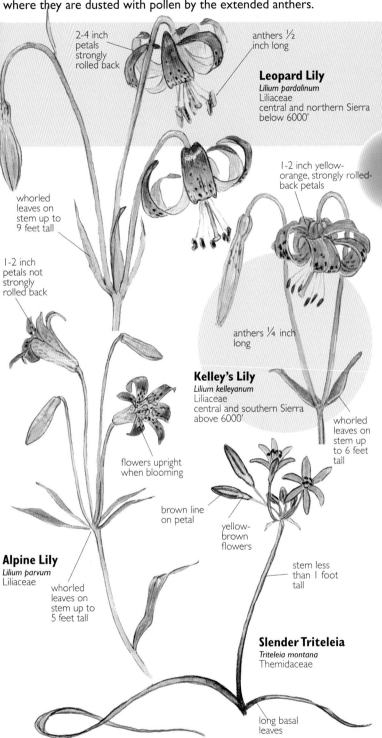

2-4 inch petals strongly rolled back

anthers ½ inch long

Leopard Lily
Lilium pardalinum
Liliaceae
central and northern Sierra
below 6000'

1-2 inch yellow-orange, strongly rolled-back petals

whorled leaves on stem up to 9 feet tall

1-2 inch petals not strongly rolled back

anthers ¼ inch long

Kelley's Lily
Lilium kelleyanum
Liliaceae
central and southern Sierra
above 6000'

whorled leaves on stem up to 6 feet tall

flowers upright when blooming

flowers upright when blooming

brown line on petal

yellow-brown flowers

Alpine Lily
Lilium parvum
Liliaceae

whorled leaves on stem up to 5 feet tall

stem less than 1 foot tall

Slender Triteleia
Triteleia montana
Themidaceae

long basal leaves

Yellow Flower Key

Choose among the groups (starting with A and AA) and follow the directions. Some species may have variable numbers of petals on different flowers, so look at several plants and flowers before starting to identify a plant.

A. Bilaterally symmetrical flowers: flowers can only be divided into similar halves along one central axis.

Go to ✿ , pages 59-62.

AA. Radially symmetrical flowers: flowers can be divided into similar halves along more than one axis. Go to B and BB below.

B. Flowers in a dense clump, making it difficult to tell the number of petals.

Go to ● , pages 63-66.

BB. Flowers not in a dense clump; you can count the number of petals per flower. Go to C below.

C. 3 petals, Go to **3** , page 67.

4 petals, Go to **4** , pages 67-68.

5 petals, Go to **5** , pages 69-72.

6 petals, Go to **6** , page 73.

Many petals or plants with variable numbers of petals on different flowers. This includes daisy- or sunflower-shaped plants.

Go to **M** , pages 74-81.

Flower Puzzles

Some flowers have complex structures that a pollinator must navigate successfully to get nectar and pollinate a flower. Once an insect learns to get nectar or pollen from a particular flower, it is likely to visit more of that same type of flower.

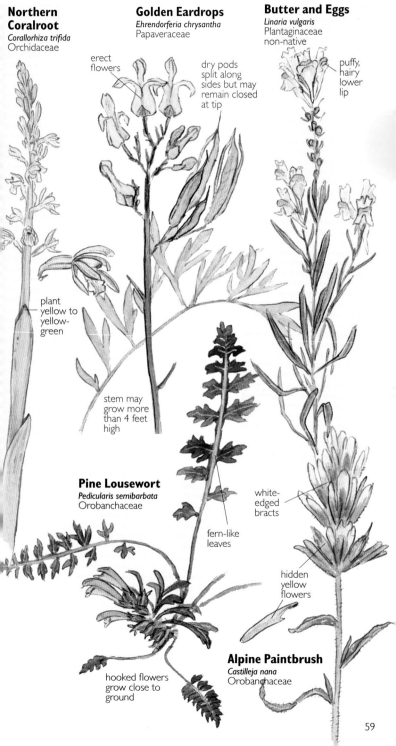

Northern Coralroot
Corallorhiza trifida
Orchidaceae

plant yellow to yellow-green

Golden Eardrops
Ehrendorferia chrysantha
Papaveraceae

erect flowers

dry pods split along sides but may remain closed at tip

stem may grow more than 4 feet high

Butter and Eggs
Linaria vulgaris
Plantaginaceae
non-native

puffy, hairy lower lip

Pine Lousewort
Pedicularis semibarbata
Orobanchaceae

fern-like leaves

hooked flowers grow close to ground

white-edged bracts

hidden yellow flowers

Alpine Paintbrush
Castilleja nana
Orobanchaceae

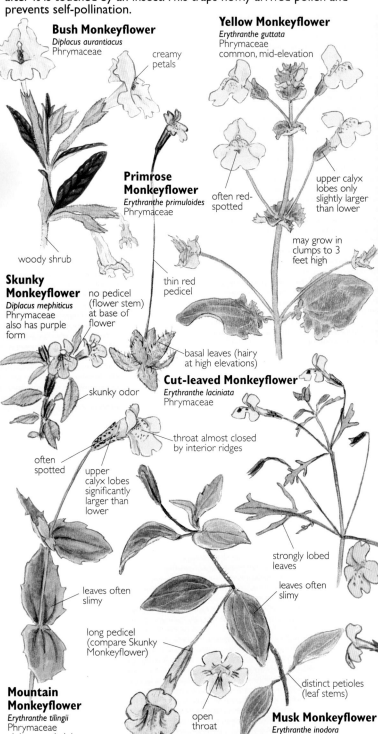

🐾 Pollen Traps

The monkeyflower stigma is touch-sensitive, closing its two lips after it is touched by an insect. This traps newly arrived pollen and prevents self-pollination.

Bush Monkeyflower
Diplacus aurantiacus
Phrymaceae

creamy petals

woody shrub

Yellow Monkeyflower
Erythranthe guttata
Phrymaceae
common, mid-elevation

often red-spotted

upper calyx lobes only slightly larger than lower

may grow in clumps to 3 feet high

Primrose Monkeyflower
Erythranthe primuloides
Phrymaceae

thin red pedicel

Skunky Monkeyflower
Diplacus mephiticus
Phrymaceae
also has purple form

no pedicel (flower stem) at base of flower

skunky odor

basal leaves (hairy at high elevations)

Cut-leaved Monkeyflower
Erythranthe laciniata
Phrymaceae

often spotted

throat almost closed by interior ridges

upper calyx lobes significantly larger than lower

strongly lobed leaves

leaves often slimy

leaves often slimy

Mountain Monkeyflower
Erythranthe tilingii
Phrymaceae
alpine or subalpine

long pedicel (compare Skunky Monkeyflower)

open throat

distinct petioles (leaf stems)

Musk Monkeyflower
Erythranthe inodora
Phrymaceae
mid-high elevation

Violets' Back-up Plan

Many violets produce two types of flowers. Large open (chasmogamous) flowers are regular blossoms that attract insects to cross-pollinate and fertilize the flower. In case no pollinators are around, violets also produce small closed (cleistogamous) flowers that self-pollinate. Both flowers produce seeds that are shot out away from the parent plant as the seed pod dries.

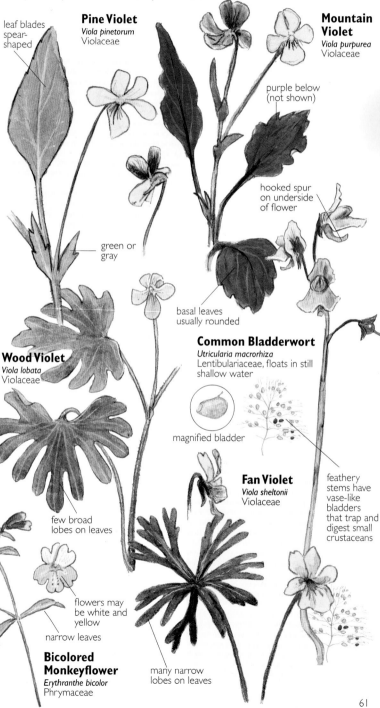

leaf blades spear-shaped

Pine Violet
Viola pinetorum
Violaceae

Mountain Violet
Viola purpurea
Violaceae

purple below (not shown)

hooked spur on underside of flower

green or gray

basal leaves usually rounded

Wood Violet
Viola lobata
Violaceae

Common Bladderwort
Utricularia macrorhiza
Lentibulariaceae, floats in still shallow water

magnified bladder

few broad lobes on leaves

Fan Violet
Viola sheltonii
Violaceae

feathery stems have vase-like bladders that trap and digest small crustaceans

flowers may be white and yellow

narrow leaves

Bicolored Monkeyflower
Erythranthe bicolor
Phrymaceae

many narrow lobes on leaves

61

Peas

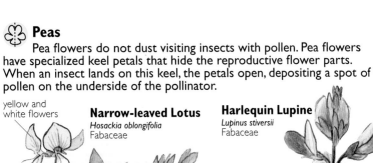

Pea flowers do not dust visiting insects with pollen. Pea flowers have specialized keel petals that hide the reproductive flower parts. When an insect lands on this keel, the petals open, depositing a spot of pollen on the underside of the pollinator.

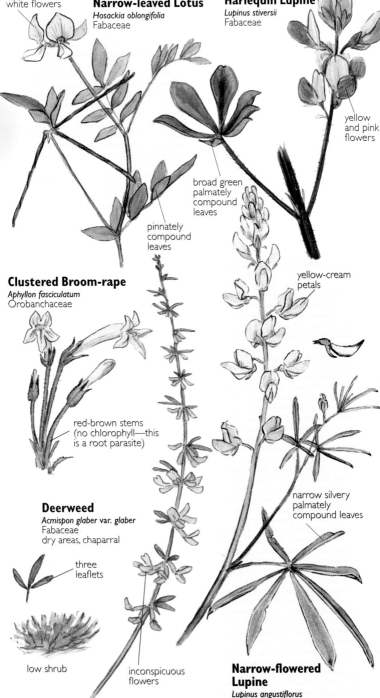

yellow and white flowers

Narrow-leaved Lotus
Hosackia oblongifolia
Fabaceae

Harlequin Lupine
Lupinus stiversii
Fabaceae

yellow and pink flowers

broad green palmately compound leaves

pinnately compound leaves

Clustered Broom-rape
Aphyllon fasciculatum
Orobanchaceae

yellow-cream petals

red-brown stems (no chlorophyll—this is a root parasite)

Deerweed
Acmispon glaber var. *glaber*
Fabaceae
dry areas, chaparral

three leaflets

narrow silvery palmately compound leaves

low shrub

inconspicuous flowers

Narrow-flowered Lupine
Lupinus angustiflorus
Fabaceae, near Mt. Lassen

Yellow Tufted Flowers

Buckwheats are an important source of food for rodents and birds living at high elevations; their flowers produce large amounts of nectar to attract bees and other insects.

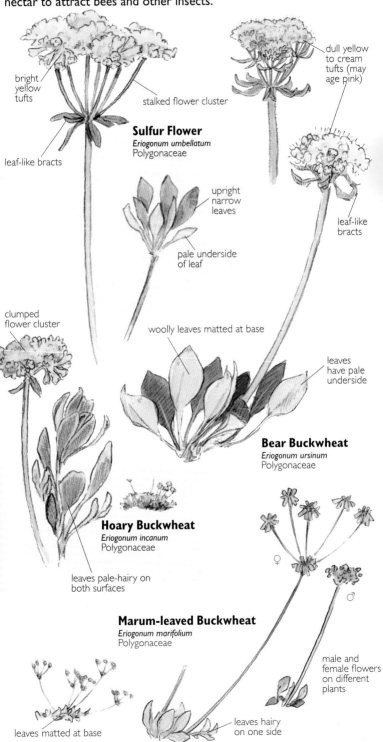

bright yellow tufts

stalked flower cluster

dull yellow to cream tufts (may age pink)

leaf-like bracts

Sulfur Flower
Eriogonum umbellatum
Polygonaceae

upright narrow leaves

pale underside of leaf

leaf-like bracts

clumped flower cluster

woolly leaves matted at base

leaves have pale underside

Bear Buckwheat
Eriogonum ursinum
Polygonaceae

Hoary Buckwheat
Eriogonum incanum
Polygonaceae

leaves pale-hairy on both surfaces

♀

♂

Marum-leaved Buckwheat
Eriogonum marifolium
Polygonaceae

male and female flowers on different plants

leaves matted at base

leaves hairy on one side

🔴 Butterfly Food

All species illustrated on this page provide important food for butterflies. Examine them carefully for caterpillars feeding among the leaves.

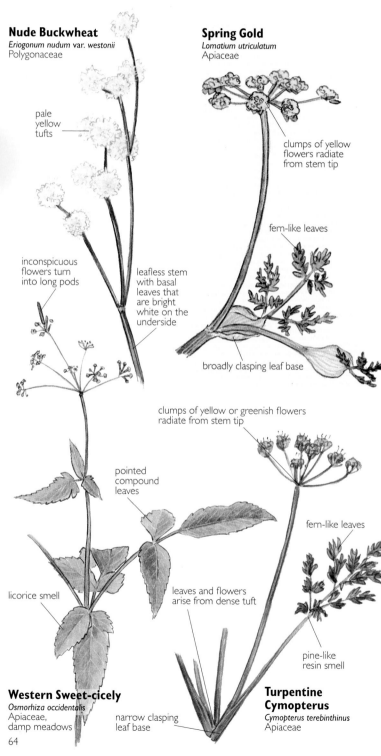

Nude Buckwheat
Eriogonum nudum var. *westonii*
Polygonaceae

pale yellow tufts

inconspicuous flowers turn into long pods

leafless stem with basal leaves that are bright white on the underside

Spring Gold
Lomatium utriculatum
Apiaceae

clumps of yellow flowers radiate from stem tip

fern-like leaves

broadly clasping leaf base

clumps of yellow or greenish flowers radiate from stem tip

pointed compound leaves

fern-like leaves

leaves and flowers arise from dense tuft

licorice smell

pine-like resin smell

Western Sweet-cicely
Osmorhiza occidentalis
Apiaceae, damp meadows

narrow clasping leaf base

Turpentine Cymopterus
Cymopterus terebinthinus
Apiaceae

Late Summer Color

Goldenrod flowers bloom late in summer and into early fall, providing late-season color and an important food source for pollen-gathering insects.

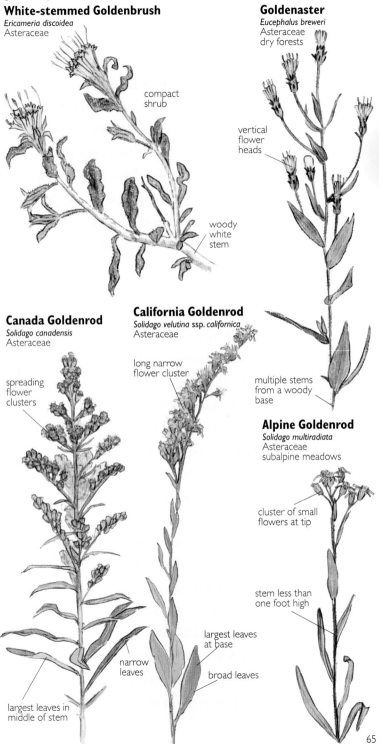

White-stemmed Goldenbrush
Ericameria discoidea
Asteraceae

compact shrub

woody white stem

Goldenaster
Eucephalus breweri
Asteraceae
dry forests

vertical flower heads

multiple stems from a woody base

Canada Goldenrod
Solidago canadensis
Asteraceae

spreading flower clusters

largest leaves in middle of stem

narrow leaves

California Goldenrod
Solidago velutina ssp. *californica*
Asteraceae

long narrow flower cluster

largest leaves at base

broad leaves

Alpine Goldenrod
Solidago multiradiata
Asteraceae
subalpine meadows

cluster of small flowers at tip

stem less than one foot high

A Threat to California's Grasslands

Yellow Star-thistle was introduced into California in the 1800s. A single plant can produce 100,000 seeds in a year. The plants have since spread, infesting over 15 million acres throughout the state. Thistles grow densely and deny soil moisture to other plants.

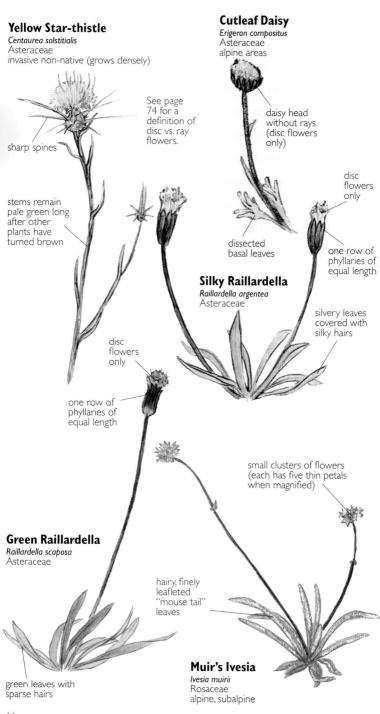

Yellow Star-thistle
Centaurea solstitialis
Asteraceae
invasive non-native (grows densely)

sharp spines

See page 74 for a definition of disc vs. ray flowers.

stems remain pale green long after other plants have turned brown

disc flowers only

one row of phyllaries of equal length

Cutleaf Daisy
Erigeron compositus
Asteraceae
alpine areas

daisy head without rays (disc flowers only)

dissected basal leaves

disc flowers only

one row of phyllaries of equal length

Silky Raillardella
Raillardella argentea
Asteraceae

silvery leaves covered with silky hairs

small clusters of flowers (each has five thin petals when magnified)

Green Raillardella
Raillardella scaposa
Asteraceae

hairy, finely leafleted "mouse tail" leaves

green leaves with sparse hairs

Muir's Ivesia
Ivesia muirii
Rosaceae
alpine, subalpine

Pollen Strings

Wet your finger and touch the stamens of large evening primrose flowers. You will find the pollen clumped in delicate strings. Touch the stigma of another primrose and you may pollinate the flower!

3 **4**

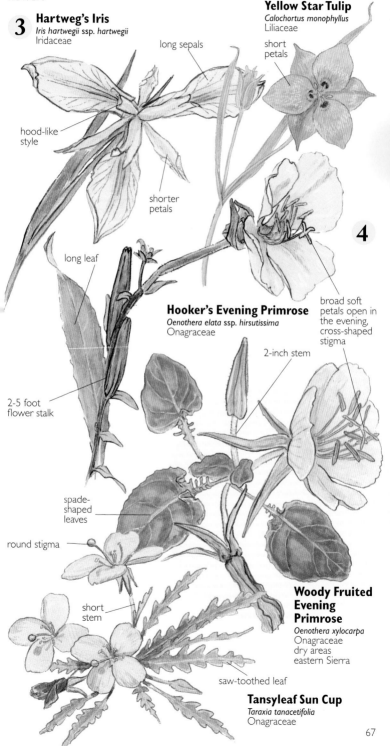

3 **Hartweg's Iris**
Iris hartwegii ssp. *hartwegii*
Iridaceae

long sepals

hood-like style

shorter petals

Yellow Star Tulip
Calochortus monophyllus
Liliaceae

short petals

4

long leaf

Hooker's Evening Primrose
Oenothera elata ssp. *hirsutissima*
Onagraceae

broad soft petals open in the evening, cross-shaped stigma

2-inch stem

2-5 foot flower stalk

spade-shaped leaves

round stigma

short stem

Woody Fruited Evening Primrose
Oenothera xylocarpa
Onagraceae
dry areas
eastern Sierra

saw-toothed leaf

Tansyleaf Sun Cup
Taraxia tanacetifolia
Onagraceae

4 Change with Elevation

The same species, found at high and low elevation, can look very different. High elevation forms are usually shorter, hairier, and more darkly pigmented—all adaptations for surviving high winds and intense solar radiation.

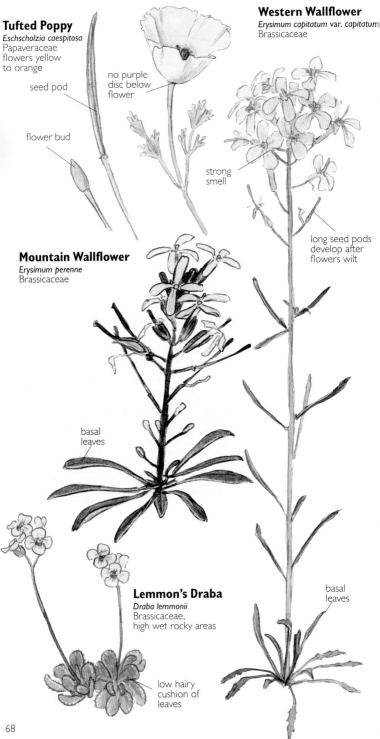

Tufted Poppy
Eschscholzia caespitosa
Papaveraceae
flowers yellow
to orange

seed pod

flower bud

no purple
disc below
flower

Western Wallflower
Erysimum capitatum var. *capitatum*
Brassicaceae

strong
smell

long seed pods
develop after
flowers wilt

Mountain Wallflower
Erysimum perenne
Brassicaceae

basal
leaves

Lemmon's Draba
Draba lemmonii
Brassicaceae,
high wet rocky areas

low hairy
cushion of
leaves

basal
leaves

Unlikely Insect Trap

Look carefully for insects trapped by the fine barbed hairs that cover the stems of *Mentzelia*. These hairs help defend the plant from herbivorous insects.

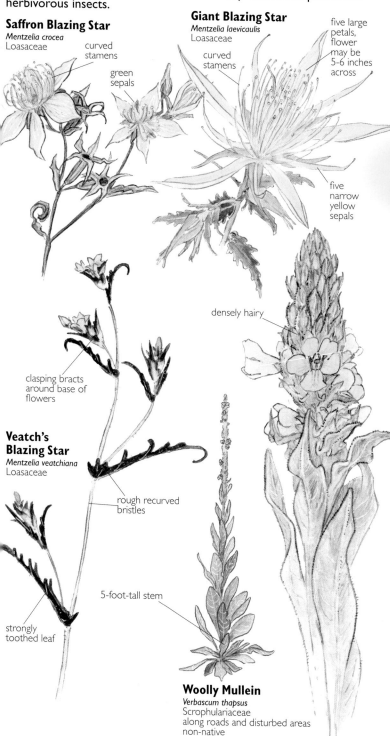

Saffron Blazing Star
Mentzelia crocea
Loasaceae

curved stamens

green sepals

Giant Blazing Star
Mentzelia laevicaulis
Loasaceae

curved stamens

five large petals, flower may be 5-6 inches across

five narrow yellow sepals

densely hairy

clasping bracts around base of flowers

Veatch's Blazing Star
Mentzelia veatchiana
Loasaceae

rough recurved bristles

strongly toothed leaf

5-foot-tall stem

Woolly Mullein
Verbascum thapsus
Scrophulariaceae
along roads and disturbed areas
non-native

5 Cinquefoil (pronounced sink-foil)

Yellow flowers stand out in the visual spectrum of day-flying insects. "Cinque" means "five" in French.

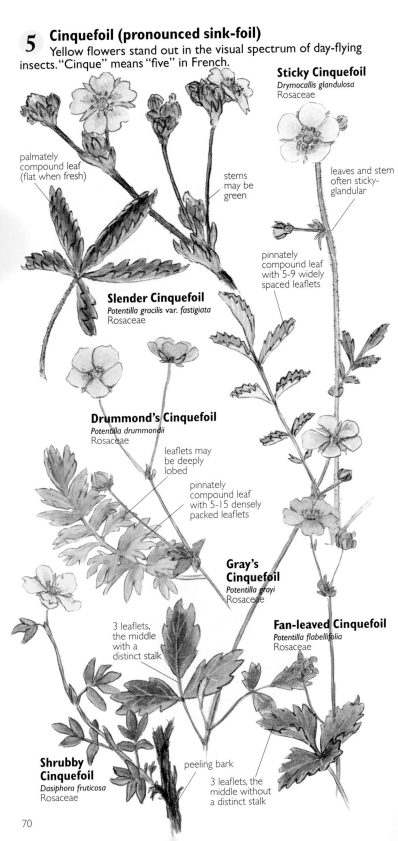

Sticky Cinquefoil
Drymocallis glandulosa
Rosaceae

leaves and stem often sticky-glandular

pinnately compound leaf with 5-9 widely spaced leaflets

palmately compound leaf (flat when fresh)

stems may be green

Slender Cinquefoil
Potentilla gracilis var. *fastigiata*
Rosaceae

Drummond's Cinquefoil
Potentilla drummondii
Rosaceae

leaflets may be deeply lobed

pinnately compound leaf with 5-15 densely packed leaflets

Gray's Cinquefoil
Potentilla grayi
Rosaceae

Fan-leaved Cinquefoil
Potentilla flabellifolia
Rosaceae

3 leaflets, the middle with a distinct stalk

Shrubby Cinquefoil
Dasiphora fruticosa
Rosaceae

peeling bark

3 leaflets, the middle without a distinct stalk

Little Frogs

Ranunculus, the buttercup genus, means "little frog" in Latin. These plants often inhabit damp areas where frogs might be found. Buttercup petals contain a layer of starch that makes the petals glossy.

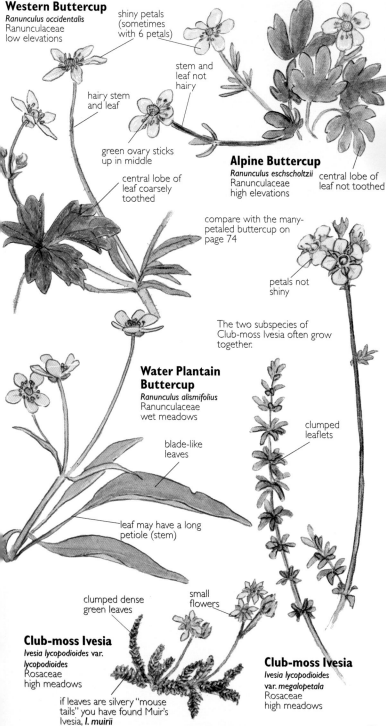

Western Buttercup
Ranunculus occidentalis
Ranunculaceae
low elevations

shiny petals (sometimes with 6 petals)

stem and leaf not hairy

hairy stem and leaf

green ovary sticks up in middle

central lobe of leaf coarsely toothed

Alpine Buttercup
Ranunculus eschscholtzii
Ranunculaceae
high elevations

central lobe of leaf not toothed

compare with the many-petaled buttercup on page 74

petals not shiny

The two subspecies of Club-moss Ivesia often grow together.

Water Plantain Buttercup
Ranunculus alismifolius
Ranunculaceae
wet meadows

blade-like leaves

clumped leaflets

leaf may have a long petiole (stem)

clumped dense green leaves

small flowers

Club-moss Ivesia
Ivesia lycopodioides var. *lycopodioides*
Rosaceae
high meadows

if leaves are silvery "mouse tails" you have found Muir's Ivesia, *I. muirii*

Club-moss Ivesia
Ivesia lycopodioides var. *megalopetala*
Rosaceae
high meadows

5 Water Storage

Stonecrop and Liveforever are adapted to store water in succulent leaves like cactus. This adaptation helps them survive at high elevations and along dry cliff walls.

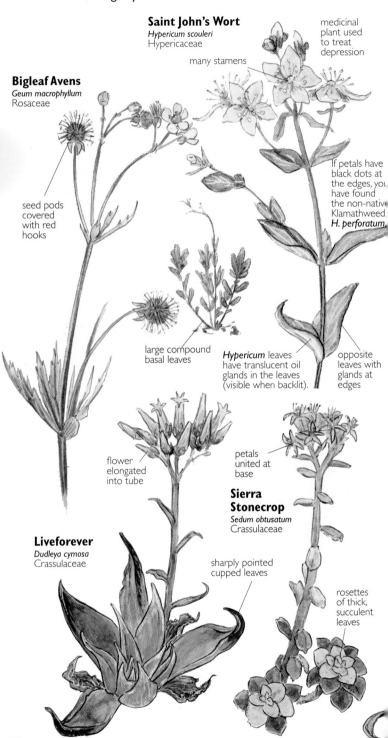

Saint John's Wort
Hypericum scouleri
Hypericaceae

medicinal plant used to treat depression

many stamens

Bigleaf Avens
Geum macrophyllum
Rosaceae

seed pods covered with red hooks

If petals have black dots at the edges, you have found the non-native Klamathweed *H. perforatum*.

large compound basal leaves

Hypericum leaves have translucent oil glands in the leaves (visible when backlit).

opposite leaves with glands at edges

flower elongated into tube

petals united at base

Sierra Stonecrop
Sedum obtusatum
Crassulaceae

Liveforever
Dudleya cymosa
Crassulaceae

sharply pointed cupped leaves

rosettes of thick, succulent leaves

Ground Nuts

Some lilies such as *Triteleia* and *Brodiaea* have edible bulbs.
California Indians who collected bulbs to eat would break off the small
accessory bulblets from the main bulb and put them in the ground. This
ensured that there would be other bulbs to eat the following year.

It is easy to confuse these bulbs
with those of the poisonous
Death Camas.

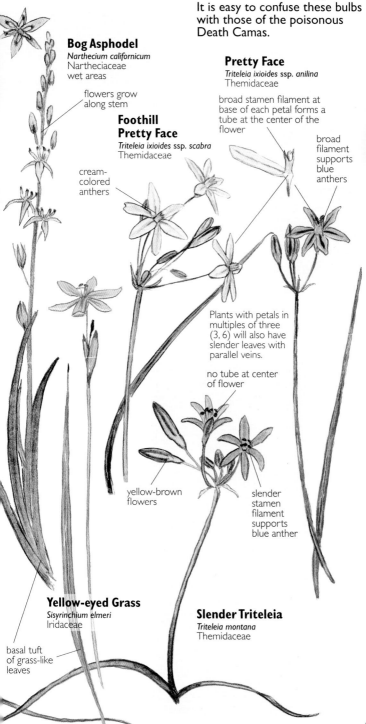

Bog Asphodel
Narthecium californicum
Nartheciaceae
wet areas

flowers grow
along stem

Pretty Face
Triteleia ixioides ssp. anilina
Themidaceae

broad stamen filament at
base of each petal forms a
tube at the center of the
flower

broad
filament
supports
blue
anthers

**Foothill
Pretty Face**
Triteleia ixioides ssp. scabra
Themidaceae

cream-
colored
anthers

Plants with petals in
multiples of three
(3, 6) will also have
slender leaves with
parallel veins.

no tube at center
of flower

yellow-brown
flowers

slender
stamen
filament
supports
blue anther

Yellow-eyed Grass
Sisyrinchium elmeri
Iridaceae

basal tuft
of grass-like
leaves

Slender Triteleia
Triteleia montana
Themidaceae

73

M Lily Pad Homes

Many aquatic invertebrates cling to floating pond-lilies. Fish use the lily pads for cover and waterfowl feast on their seeds in late summer.

Yellow Pond-lily
Nuphar polysepala
Nymphaeaceae

California Buttercup
Ranunculus californicus
Ranunculaceae

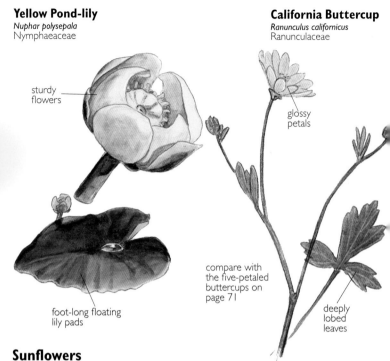

sturdy flowers

glossy petals

compare with the five-petaled buttercups on page 71

foot-long floating lily pads

deeply lobed leaves

Sunflowers

How many petals does a sunflower have? Be careful, it's a trick question. Five per flower. Flowers in the family Asteraceae are dense heads of many small flowers. Look at a flower head carefully with a magnifying glass. The long petals on the outside are "ray flowers"— five petals fused into one long petal (you can sometimes see five serrations on the tip). The small bumps in the middle of the flower are "disc flowers"— with five tiny petals.

ray flowers made from fused petals

Some flower heads are made entirely of ray flowers or disc flowers.

disc flowers bloom first at the edge of the head and progress to the center

head with ray flowers only (see page 81)

head with disc flowers only (see page 66)

74

Big Yellow Sunflowers
How could you help but pollinate something this beautiful?

Woolly Mule's Ears
Wyethia mollis
Asteraceae

leaves densely woolly

flowers same height as leaves

leaves covered with dense hairs, giving leaves gray cast

leaf bases taper abruptly to midvein

Arrow-leaved Balsam-root
Balsamorhiza sagittata
Asteraceae

flowers taller than leaves

triangular leaves, lobed at base

Common Sunflower
Helianthus annuus
Asteraceae
disturbed areas,
Yosemite Valley

Narrow-leaved Mule's Ears
Wyethia angustifolia
Asteraceae

may have hairs but not densely woolly

2-6 foot stem with many heads

leaf bases taper gradually to midvein

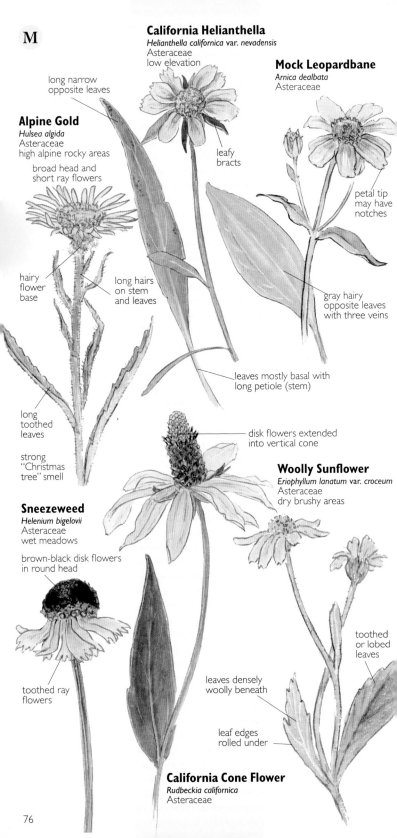

M

California Helianthella
Helianthella californica var. *nevadensis*
Asteraceae
low elevation

Mock Leopardbane
Arnica dealbata
Asteraceae

long narrow
opposite leaves

Alpine Gold
Hulsea algida
Asteraceae
high alpine rocky areas

broad head and
short ray flowers

leafy
bracts

petal tip
may have
notches

hairy
flower
base

long hairs
on stem
and leaves

gray hairy
opposite leaves
with three veins

long
toothed
leaves

leaves mostly basal with
long petiole (stem)

strong
"Christmas
tree" smell

disk flowers extended
into vertical cone

Woolly Sunflower
Eriophyllum lanatum var. *croceum*
Asteraceae
dry brushy areas

Sneezeweed
Helenium bigelovii
Asteraceae
wet meadows

brown-black disk flowers
in round head

toothed
or lobed
leaves

toothed ray
flowers

leaves densely
woolly beneath

leaf edges
rolled under

California Cone Flower
Rudbeckia californica
Asteraceae

Difficulty Identifying Arnica? Relax, It's Not You...

Arnicas are tough to identify. Some species hybridize and some populations reproduce asexually and have unique features.

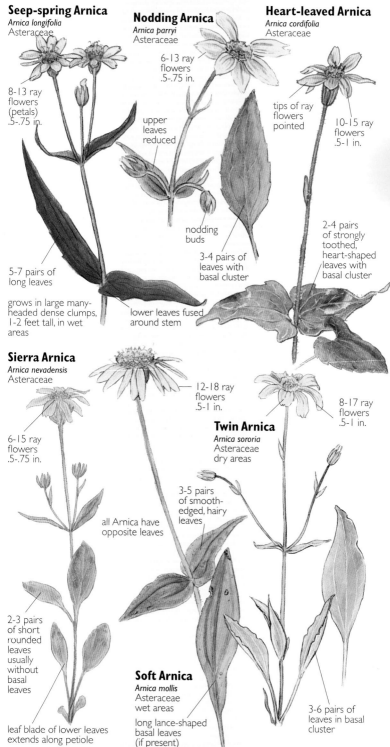

Seep-spring Arnica
Arnica longifolia
Asteraceae

8-13 ray flowers (petals) .5-.75 in.

5-7 pairs of long leaves

grows in large many-headed dense clumps, 1-2 feet tall, in wet areas

Nodding Arnica
Arnica parryi
Asteraceae

6-13 ray flowers .5-.75 in.

upper leaves reduced

nodding buds

3-4 pairs of leaves with basal cluster

lower leaves fused around stem

Heart-leaved Arnica
Arnica cordifolia
Asteraceae

tips of ray flowers pointed

10-15 ray flowers .5-1 in.

2-4 pairs of strongly toothed, heart-shaped leaves with basal cluster

Sierra Arnica
Arnica nevadensis
Asteraceae

6-15 ray flowers .5-.75 in.

12-18 ray flowers .5-1 in.

all Arnica have opposite leaves

2-3 pairs of short rounded leaves usually without basal leaves

leaf blade of lower leaves extends along petiole

Twin Arnica
Arnica sororia
Asteraceae
dry areas

8-17 ray flowers .5-1 in.

3-5 pairs of smooth-edged, hairy leaves

Soft Arnica
Arnica mollis
Asteraceae
wet areas

long lance-shaped basal leaves (if present)

3-6 pairs of leaves in basal cluster

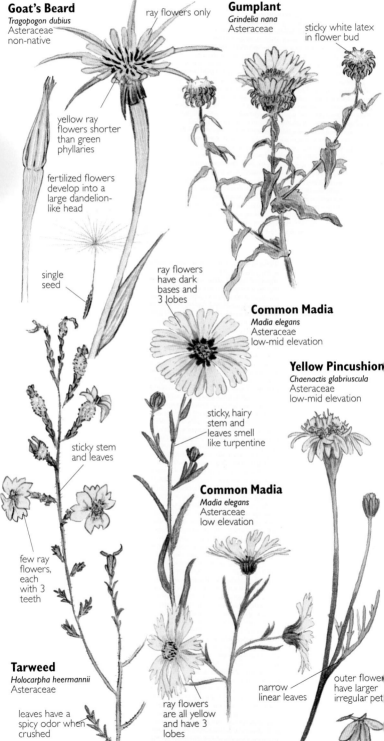

M Plenty of Pollen

Most sunflowers produce abundant pollen and provide a large landing platform. This makes them very attractive to pollinators.

Goat's Beard
Tragopogon dubius
Asteraceae
non-native

ray flowers only

yellow ray flowers shorter than green phyllaries

fertilized flowers develop into a large dandelion-like head

single seed

Gumplant
Grindelia nana
Asteraceae

sticky white latex in flower bud

ray flowers have dark bases and 3 lobes

Common Madia
Madia elegans
Asteraceae
low-mid elevation

Yellow Pincushion
Chaenactis glabriuscula
Asteraceae
low-mid elevation

sticky stem and leaves

sticky, hairy stem and leaves smell like turpentine

Common Madia
Madia elegans
Asteraceae
low elevation

few ray flowers, each with 3 teeth

Tarweed
Holocarpha heermannii
Asteraceae

leaves have a spicy odor when crushed

ray flowers are all yellow and have 3 lobes

narrow linear leaves

outer flower have larger irregular pet

Goldenrod vs. Groundsel

Groundsels have large flowers and phyllaries in one row that distinguish them from Goldenrod, which has small flowers with several rows of phyllaries. These plants are great places to look for crab spiders.

M

phyllaries in one row (all equal size)

Canada Goldenrod
Solidago canadensis
Asteraceae

spreading flower clusters

narrow leaves

largest leaves in middle

broad leaves

California Goldenrod
Solidago velutina ssp. *californica*
Asteraceae

long narrow flower cluster

cluster of small flowers at tip

short stem

leaves smooth or toothed

largest leaves at base

Alpine Goldenrod
Solidago multiradiata
Asteraceae
subalpine meadows

basal leaves

Alpine Groundsel
Packera werneriifolia
Asteraceae

Sierra Ragwort
Senecio scorzonella
Asteraceae
subalpine meadows

phyllaries have black tips

ray flowers often absent

leaf widest near tip

Mountain Butterweed
Senecio integerrimus
Asteraceae

fuzzy leaves

ray and disc flowers

common and highly variable

Arrowleaf Groundsel
Senecio triangularis
Asteraceae

triangular leaves

79

M Summer Drought

Thin alpine soil does not hold much water. High-elevation species must adapt to withstand dry conditions, intense sunlight, extremes in temperature, and strong winds.

Pumice Hulsea

Hulsea vestita
Asteraceae
southern Sierra

3 small teeth at tip of ray flower

short stems at high elevation

flowers may be tinged purple

woody base

woolly leaves with 3-5 teeth

roundish leaves in dense woolly rosette

Woolly Sunflower

Eriophyllum lanatum var. integrifolium
Asteraceae
rocky ridges, mid-high elevation

Shaggy Hawkweed

Hieracium horridum
Asteraceae
rocky areas

flowers in tight cluster

4-6 short ray flowers per flower

ray flowers only

Bush Groundsel

Senecio flaccidus var. douglasii
Asteraceae

long hairs

leaves covered with dense white hairs

woolly deeply lobed leaves

leaves thread-like or with lobes on sides

woody shrub

milky sap

Golden Yarrow

Eriophyllum confertiflorum
Asteraceae
open, dry slopes, low-mid elevation

80

Dandelion-like Flowers

Dandelions have been used as traditional cures for a variety of ailments from warts to kidney problems. "Officinale" in a scientific name indicates that the plant was thought to have medicinal uses.

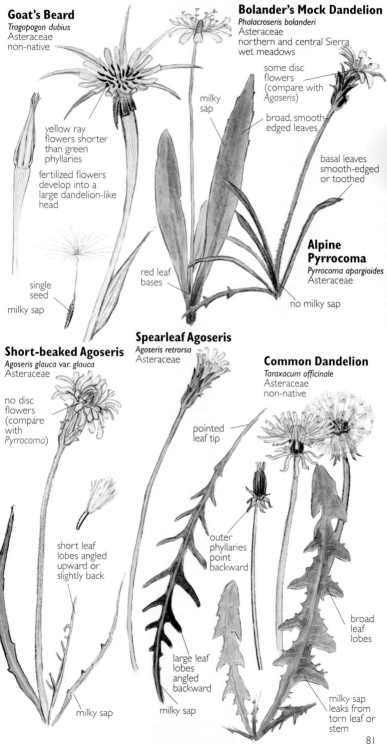

Goat's Beard
Tragopogon dubius
Asteraceae
non-native

yellow ray flowers shorter than green phyllaries

fertilized flowers develop into a large dandelion-like head

single seed

milky sap

Bolander's Mock Dandelion
Phalacroseris bolanderi
Asteraceae
northern and central Sierra
wet meadows

some disc flowers (compare with *Agoseris*)

broad, smooth-edged leaves

milky sap

basal leaves smooth-edged or toothed

Alpine Pyrrocoma
Pyrrocoma apargioides
Asteraceae

no milky sap

red leaf bases

Short-beaked Agoseris
Agoseris glauca var. *glauca*
Asteraceae

no disc flowers (compare with *Pyrrocoma*)

short leaf lobes angled upward or slightly back

milky sap

Spearleaf Agoseris
Agoseris retrorsa
Asteraceae

pointed leaf tip

outer phyllaries point backward

large leaf lobes angled backward

milky sap

Common Dandelion
Taraxacum officinale
Asteraceae
non-native

broad leaf lobes

milky sap leaks from torn leaf or stem

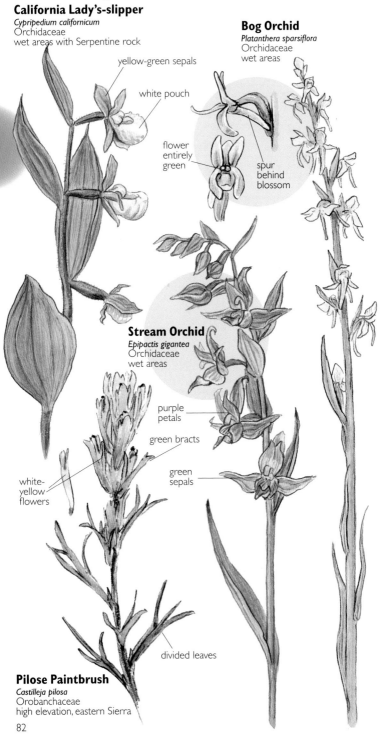

Growing Together

Orchids have some of the most complex co-evolved relationships with insect pollinators. They also have complex relationships with soil fungi, making them difficult to transplant. Enjoy these beautiful species without disturbing them.

California Lady's-slipper
Cypripedium californicum
Orchidaceae
wet areas with Serpentine rock

yellow-green sepals

white pouch

Bog Orchid
Platanthera sparsiflora
Orchidaceae
wet areas

flower entirely green

spur behind blossom

Stream Orchid
Epipactis gigantea
Orchidaceae
wet areas

purple petals

green bracts

green sepals

white-yellow flowers

divided leaves

Pilose Paintbrush
Castilleja pilosa
Orobanchaceae
high elevation, eastern Sierra

Green Flowers

Not all flowers are pollinated by insects. Some, such as Meadow-rue and grasses, are wind-pollinated and do not need showy petals to attract insects.

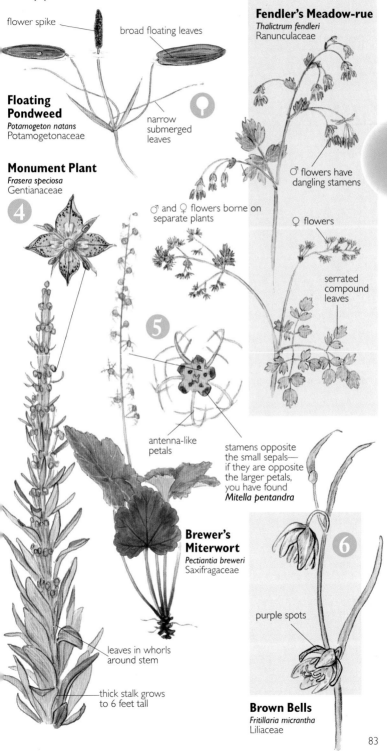

flower spike

broad floating leaves

Floating Pondweed
Potamogeton natans
Potamogetonaceae

narrow submerged leaves

Fendler's Meadow-rue
Thalictrum fendleri
Ranunculaceae

♂ flowers have dangling stamens

♀ flowers

serrated compound leaves

Monument Plant
Frasera speciosa
Gentianaceae

♂ and ♀ flowers borne on separate plants

antenna-like petals

stamens opposite the small sepals—if they are opposite the larger petals, you have found *Mitella pentandra*

Brewer's Miterwort
Pectiantia breweri
Saxifragaceae

leaves in whorls around stem

thick stalk grows to 6 feet tall

purple spots

Brown Bells
Fritillaria micrantha
Liliaceae

Blue-purple Flower Key

Choose among the groups (starting with A and AA) and follow the directions. Some species may have variable numbers of petals on different flowers, so look at several plants and flowers before starting to identify a plant.

A. Bilaterally symmetrical flowers: flowers can only be divided into similar halves along one central axis.

Go to , pages 85-95.

AA. Radially symmetrical flowers: flowers can be divided into similar halves along more than one axis. Go to B and BB below.

B. Flowers in a dense clump, making it difficult to tell the number of petals.

Go to , page 96.

BB. Flowers not in a dense clump; you can count the number of petals per flower. Go to C below.

C.   3 petals, Go to **3**, page 97.

       4 petals, Go to **4**, page 98.

       5 petals, Go to **5**, pages 98-102.

       6 petals, Go to **6**, pages 102-103.

Many petals or plants with variable numbers of petals on different flowers. This includes daisy- or sunflower-shaped plants.
       Go to **M**, pages 104-105.

Alternate Leaves, Deadly Beauty

Monkshood contains the powerful alkaloid aconitine that paralyzes the nervous system. Foxglove contains the cardiac glycoside digitoxin, an important heart medicine but deadly in higher concentrations.

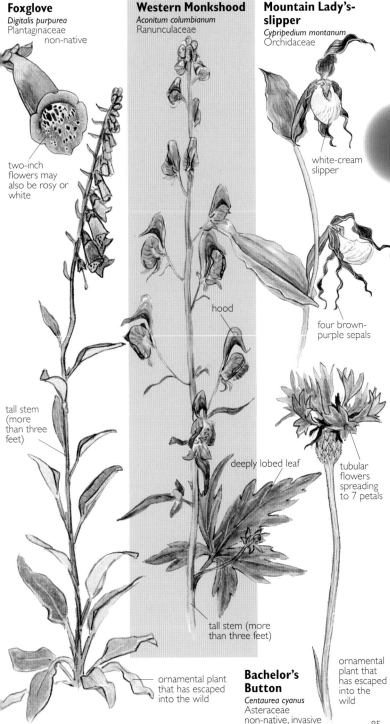

Foxglove
Digitalis purpurea
Plantaginaceae
non-native

two-inch flowers may also be rosy or white

tall stem (more than three feet)

ornamental plant that has escaped into the wild

Western Monkshood
Aconitum columbianum
Ranunculaceae

hood

deeply lobed leaf

tall stem (more than three feet)

Mountain Lady's-slipper
Cypripedium montanum
Orchidaceae

white-cream slipper

four brown-purple sepals

tubular flowers spreading to 7 petals

ornamental plant that has escaped into the wild

Bachelor's Button
Centaurea cyanus
Asteraceae
non-native, invasive

85

Alternate Leaves, Larkspur Grazing Defenses

Larkspurs contain poisonous alkaloids that can paralyze the hearts of cattle, horses, or sheep that eat young plants.

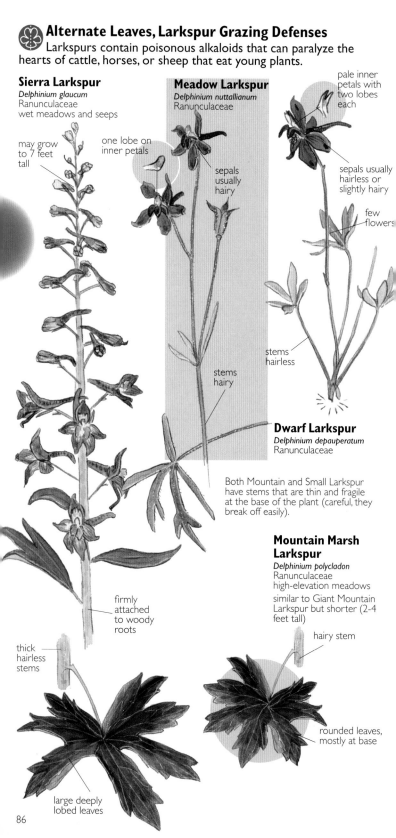

Sierra Larkspur
Delphinium glaucum
Ranunculaceae
wet meadows and seeps

may grow to 7 feet tall

one lobe on inner petals

Meadow Larkspur
Delphinium nuttallianum
Ranunculaceae

sepals usually hairy

pale inner petals with two lobes each

sepals usually hairless or slightly hairy

few flowers

stems hairy

stems hairless

Dwarf Larkspur
Delphinium depauperatum
Ranunculaceae

Both Mountain and Small Larkspur have stems that are thin and fragile at the base of the plant (careful, they break off easily).

Mountain Marsh Larkspur
Delphinium polycladon
Ranunculaceae
high-elevation meadows

similar to Giant Mountain Larkspur but shorter (2-4 feet tall)

firmly attached to woody roots

hairy stem

thick hairless stems

rounded leaves, mostly at base

large deeply lobed leaves

Alternate Leaves, Indian Paintbrush

Paintbrushes are partially parasitic on the roots of neighboring plants such as sagebrush.

Alpine Paintbrush

Castilleja nana
Orobanchaceae
dry, rocky areas
from Lake Tahoe south

dull sepals
and bracts

bracts with
greenish tips

upper lip
of flower
purplish

Lemmon's Paintbrush

Castilleja lemmonii
Orobanchaceae
wet areas

pink-purple
sepals and
bracts

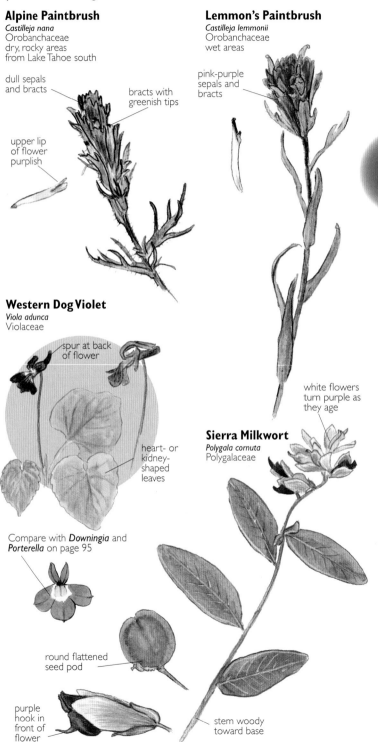

Western Dog Violet

Viola adunca
Violaceae

spur at back
of flower

heart- or
kidney-
shaped
leaves

Compare with *Downingia* and *Porterella* on page 95

white flowers
turn purple as
they age

Sierra Milkwort

Polygala cornuta
Polygalaceae

round flattened
seed pod

stem woody
toward base

purple
hook in
front of
flower

87

Narrow Palmately Compound Leaves: Lupine

Hidden inside lupine side petals is a pale, canoe-shaped petal called a keel that protects the stamens and pistils. The keel is an important identification feature. Is it strongly hooked? Are there fine hairs on the top edge?

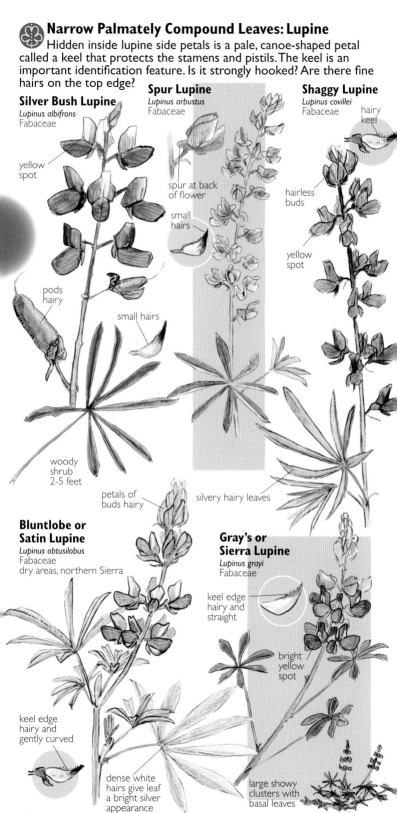

Silver Bush Lupine
Lupinus albifrons
Fabaceae

yellow spot

pods hairy

small hairs

woody shrub 2-5 feet

Spur Lupine
Lupinus arbustus
Fabaceae

spur at back of flower

small hairs

petals of buds hairy

silvery hairy leaves

Shaggy Lupine
Lupinus covillei
Fabaceae

hairy keel

hairless buds

yellow spot

Bluntlobe or Satin Lupine
Lupinus obtusilobus
Fabaceae
dry areas, northern Sierra

keel edge hairy and gently curved

dense white hairs give leaf a bright silver appearance

Gray's or Sierra Lupine
Lupinus grayi
Fabaceae

keel edge hairy and straight

bright yellow spot

large showy clusters with basal leaves

Broad Palmately Compound Leaves: Lupine

Lower flowers on lupine plants often have darker colors on the upright banner petal. This color change occurs after pollination, signaling potential pollinators to visit the upper flowers instead of those that have already been visited by an insect.

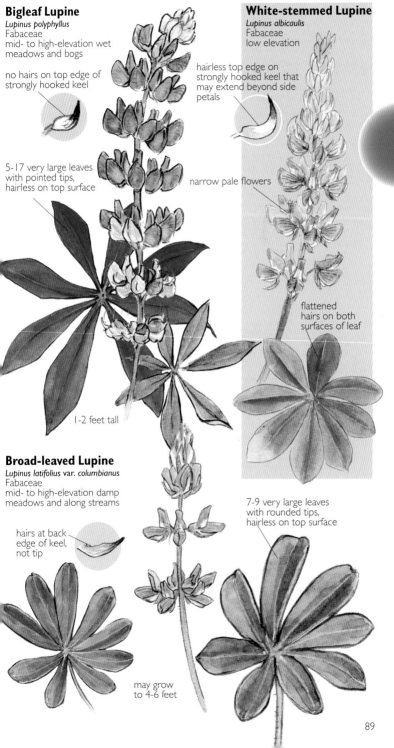

Bigleaf Lupine
Lupinus polyphyllus
Fabaceae
mid- to high-elevation wet meadows and bogs

no hairs on top edge of strongly hooked keel

5-17 very large leaves with pointed tips, hairless on top surface

1-2 feet tall

White-stemmed Lupine
Lupinus albicaulis
Fabaceae
low elevation

hairless top edge on strongly hooked keel that may extend beyond side petals

narrow pale flowers

flattened hairs on both surfaces of leaf

Broad-leaved Lupine
Lupinus latifolius var. *columbianus*
Fabaceae
mid- to high-elevation damp meadows and along streams

hairs at back edge of keel, not tip

7-9 very large leaves with rounded tips, hairless on top surface

may grow to 4-6 feet

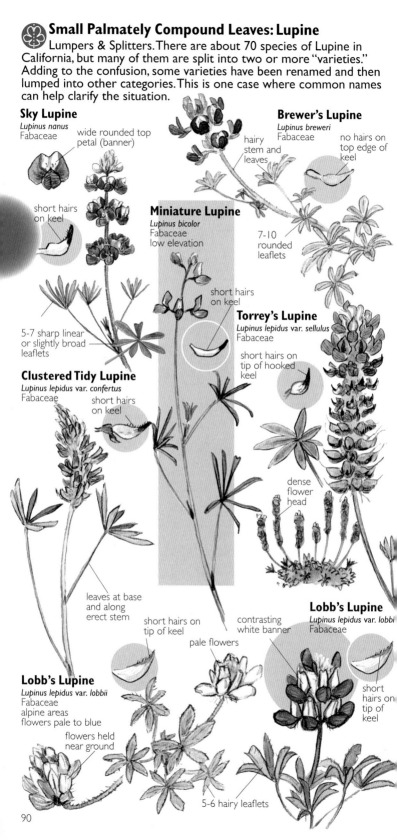

Small Palmately Compound Leaves: Lupine

Lumpers & Splitters. There are about 70 species of Lupine in California, but many of them are split into two or more "varieties." Adding to the confusion, some varieties have been renamed and then lumped into other categories. This is one case where common names can help clarify the situation.

Sky Lupine
Lupinus nanus
Fabaceae

wide rounded top petal (banner)

short hairs on keel

5-7 sharp linear or slightly broad leaflets

Brewer's Lupine
Lupinus breweri
Fabaceae

hairy stem and leaves

no hairs on top edge of keel

7-10 rounded leaflets

Miniature Lupine
Lupinus bicolor
Fabaceae
low elevation

short hairs on keel

Torrey's Lupine
Lupinus lepidus var. *sellulus*
Fabaceae

short hairs on tip of hooked keel

Clustered Tidy Lupine
Lupinus lepidus var. *confertus*
Fabaceae

short hairs on keel

dense flower head

leaves at base and along erect stem

Lobb's Lupine
Lupinus lepidus var. *lobbii*
Fabaceae
alpine areas
flowers pale to blue

flowers held near ground

short hairs on tip of keel

pale flowers

contrasting white banner

Lobb's Lupine
Lupinus lepidus var. *lobbii*
Fabaceae

short hairs on tip of keel

5-6 hairy leaflets

Pinnately Compound Leaves

Plants in the pea family (Fabaceae) survive in poor soil because they have small bumps, or nodules, on their roots that provide a home for bacteria that extract nitrogen from the air and transform it to a form the plant can use.

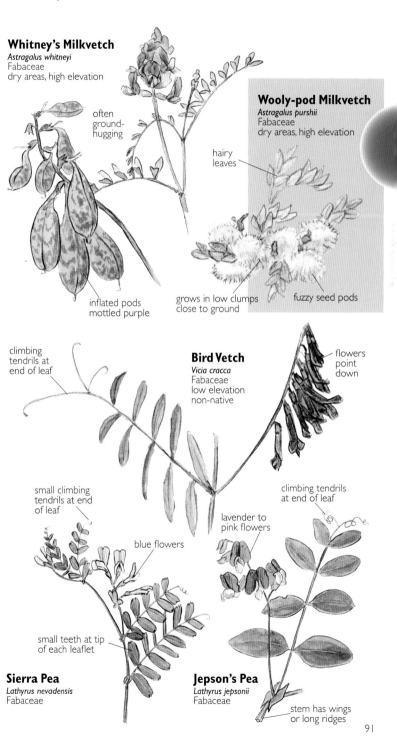

Whitney's Milkvetch
Astragalus whitneyi
Fabaceae
dry areas, high elevation

often ground-hugging

Wooly-pod Milkvetch
Astragalus purshii
Fabaceae
dry areas, high elevation

hairy leaves

inflated pods mottled purple

grows in low clumps close to ground

fuzzy seed pods

climbing tendrils at end of leaf

Bird Vetch
Vicia cracca
Fabaceae
low elevation
non-native

flowers point down

small climbing tendrils at end of leaf

blue flowers

lavender to pink flowers

climbing tendrils at end of leaf

small teeth at tip of each leaflet

Sierra Pea
Lathyrus nevadensis
Fabaceae

Jepson's Pea
Lathyrus jepsonii
Fabaceae

stem has wings or long ridges

Opposite Leaves, Tubular Flowers

Showy Penstemon
Penstemon speciosus
Plantaginaceae

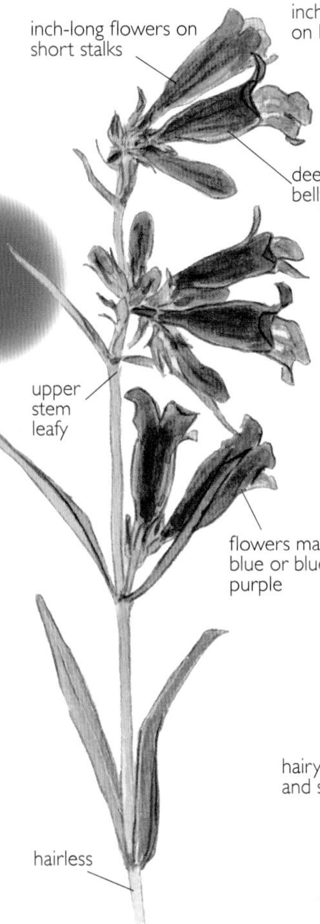

inch-long flowers on short stalks

deep belly

upper stem leafy

flowers may be blue or blue-purple

hairless

Mountain Blue Penstemon
Penstemon laetus
Plantaginaceae

inch-long flowers on long stalks

stem often dirty (resin catches dirt)

woody base

hairy leaves and stem

Grayleaf Skullcap
Scutellaria siphocampyloides
Lamiaceae
low elevation

flower white at base

square stem

Slender Penstemon
Penstemon gracilentus
Plantaginaceae

clusters of half-inch-long flowers on long stalks

narrow leaves

Davidson's Penstemon
Penstemon davidsonii
Plantaginaceae
high elevation

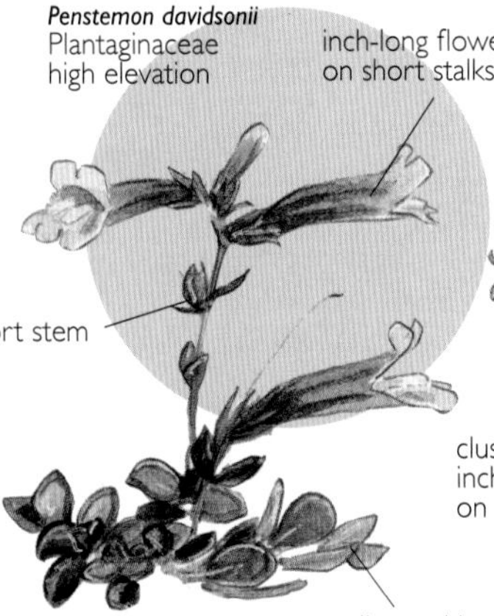

inch-long flowers on short stalks

short stem

small round leaves

Opposite Leaves, Tubular Flowers

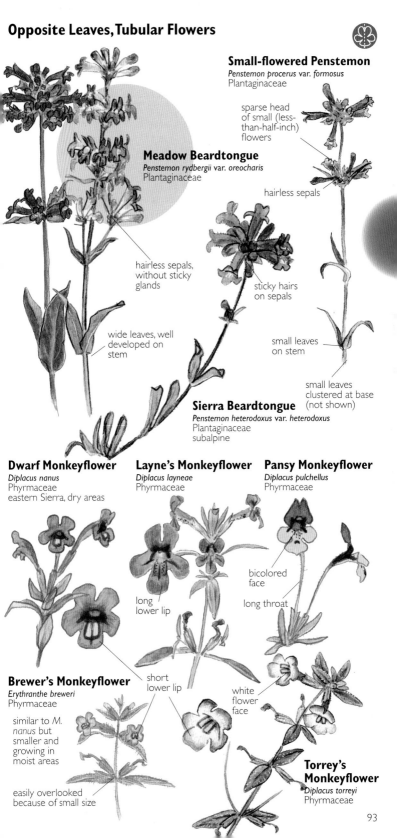

Small-flowered Penstemon
Penstemon procerus var. *formosus*
Plantaginaceae

sparse head of small (less-than-half-inch) flowers

hairless sepals

Meadow Beardtongue
Penstemon rydbergii var. *oreocharis*
Plantaginaceae

hairless sepals, without sticky glands

sticky hairs on sepals

wide leaves, well developed on stem

small leaves on stem

small leaves clustered at base (not shown)

Sierra Beardtongue
Penstemon heterodoxus var. *heterodoxus*
Plantaginaceae
subalpine

Dwarf Monkeyflower
Diplacus nanus
Phyrmaceae
eastern Sierra, dry areas

Layne's Monkeyflower
Diplacus layneae
Phyrmaceae

Pansy Monkeyflower
Diplacus pulchellus
Phyrmaceae

bicolored face

long throat

long lower lip

Brewer's Monkeyflower
Erythranthe breweri
Phyrmaceae

similar to *M. nanus* but smaller and growing in moist areas

short lower lip

white flower face

easily overlooked because of small size

Torrey's Monkeyflower
Diplacus torreyi
Phyrmaceae

Opposite Leaves, Flowers Spreading

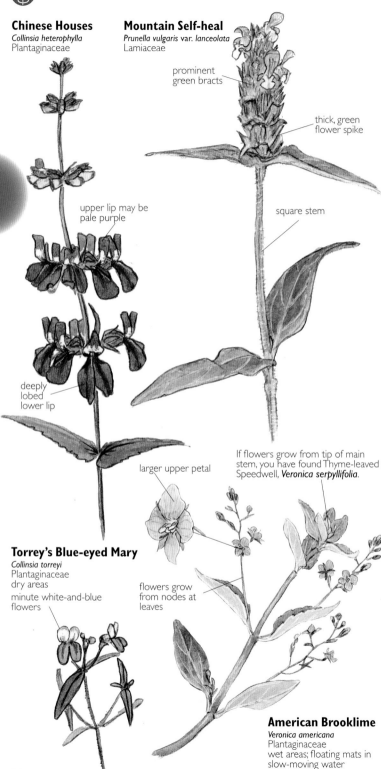

Chinese Houses
Collinsia heterophylla
Plantaginaceae

upper lip may be pale purple

deeply lobed lower lip

Mountain Self-heal
Prunella vulgaris var. *lanceolata*
Lamiaceae

prominent green bracts

thick, green flower spike

square stem

If flowers grow from tip of main stem, you have found Thyme-leaved Speedwell, *Veronica serpyllifolia*.

larger upper petal

Torrey's Blue-eyed Mary
Collinsia torreyi
Plantaginaceae
dry areas
minute white-and-blue flowers

flowers grow from nodes at leaves

American Brooklime
Veronica americana
Plantaginaceae
wet areas; floating mats in slow-moving water

Opposite Leaves, Flowers Spreading with Minty Smell

Mountain Pennyroyal
Monardella odoratissima ssp. *glauca*
Lamiaceae

reddish-purple flowers

one layer of purple bracts below flower cluster

square stem

hairy stem and leaves

Mustang Mint
Monardella breweri ssp. *lanceolata*
Lamiaceae

pale purple flowers

silvery haired leaves near top of plant

one layer of straw-colored papery bracts below flower cluster

densely hairy, mostly leafless square stem

pale purple flowers

two layers of green or purple bracts below flower cluster

Mountain Monardella
Monardella odoratissima
Lamiaceae

may be hairless

square stem

long stem-like ovary

Bach's Downingia
Downingia bacigalupii
Campanulaceae
low-elevation wet meadows
over 6 inches high

Sierra Downingia
Downingia montana
Campanulaceae
low-elevation wet meadows
less than 6 inches high
yellow only in throat

Porterella
Porterella carnosula
Campanulaceae
high-elevation wet meadows
or vernal pools

short ovary on long stem

less than 6 inches high

compare with *Viola*, p. 87

yellow eye

95

Dense Heads of Small Flowers

While the spiny heads of thistles are well protected from deer and other herbivores, they are a banquet for goldfinches and other seed-eating birds that can perch above the spines and clear away the down (hairs attached to seeds) to expose oil-rich seeds.

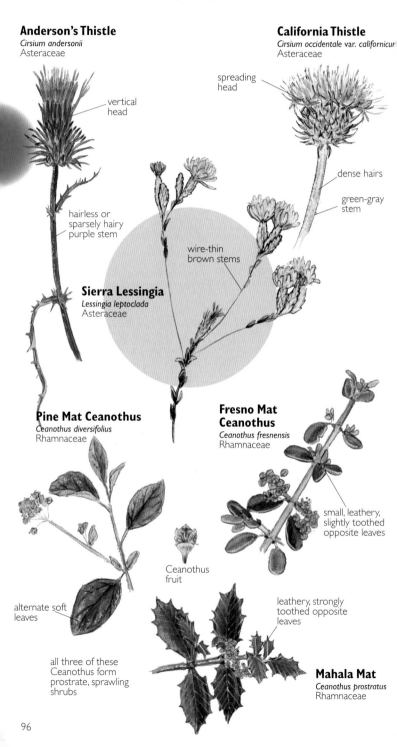

Anderson's Thistle
Cirsium andersonii
Asteraceae

vertical head

hairless or sparsely hairy purple stem

California Thistle
Cirsium occidentale var. californicum
Asteraceae

spreading head

dense hairs

green-gray stem

Sierra Lessingia
Lessingia leptoclada
Asteraceae

wire-thin brown stems

Pine Mat Ceanothus
Ceanothus diversifolius
Rhamnaceae

Fresno Mat Ceanothus
Ceanothus fresnensis
Rhamnaceae

small, leathery, slightly toothed opposite leaves

Ceanothus fruit

alternate soft leaves

leathery, strongly toothed opposite leaves

all three of these Ceanothus form prostrate, sprawling shrubs

Mahala Mat
Ceanothus prostratus
Rhamnaceae

Fooling with Fungus Flies

Wild ginger plants are pollinated by fungus flies that mistake the flowers for the mushrooms on which they lay their eggs.

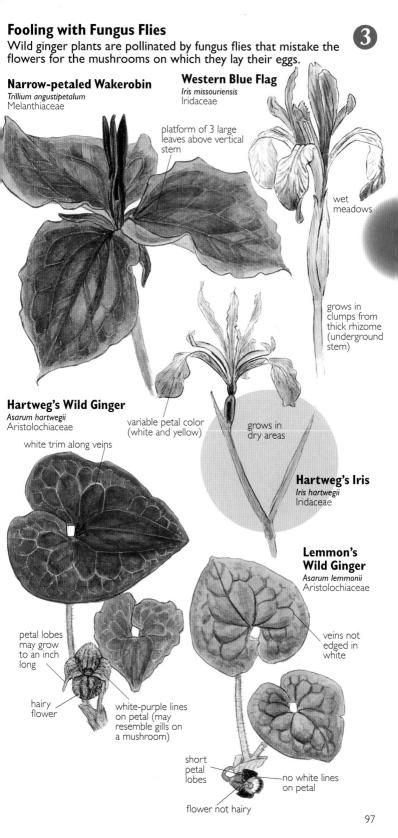

Narrow-petaled Wakerobin
Trillium angustipetalum
Melanthiaceae

platform of 3 large leaves above vertical stem

Western Blue Flag
Iris missouriensis
Iridaceae

wet meadows

grows in clumps from thick rhizome (underground stem)

Hartweg's Wild Ginger
Asarum hartwegii
Aristolochiaceae

white trim along veins

variable petal color (white and yellow)

grows in dry areas

Hartweg's Iris
Iris hartwegii
Iridaceae

Lemmon's Wild Ginger
Asarum lemmonii
Aristolochiaceae

veins not edged in white

petal lobes may grow to an inch long

hairy flower

white-purple lines on petal (may resemble gills on a mushroom)

short petal lobes

no white lines on petal

flower not hairy

97

4 5 Insect-Eating Plants

Pitcher plants have uniquely adapted leaves to trap and digest insects. The hollow leaves contain water and bacteria to digest the insects that fly inside. Digested insects provide nutrients, not energy. Pitcher plant leaves make sugar from sunlight just like other species of plants.

4 Sierra Gentian
Gentianopsis holopetala
Gentianaceae

smooth petal edge

petal shorter than flower tube

Hiker's Gentian
Gentianopsis simplex
Gentianaceae

fringed petal edge

petal slightly twisted

petal as long as flower tube

Arching Rock Cress
Boechera arcuata
Brassicaceae

red-purple cross-shaped flower

curved fruits (siliques) hang down

long gray leaves at base of 2-foot-tall stem

5

Transparent windows at top make insects look for an exit in the wrong place while luring them deeper into the plant.

The inside of the tube is lined with downward-facing hairs. Once an insect starts down, there is only one way to go...

cobra-shaped leaf

green sepals

purple petals

Purple Milkweed
Asclepias cordifolia
Apocynaceae

seed pod

hairless opposite leaves (leaks milky latex if damaged). Compare with Showy Milkweed on p. 46

California Pitcher Plant
Darlingtonia californica
Sarraceniaceae
wet areas

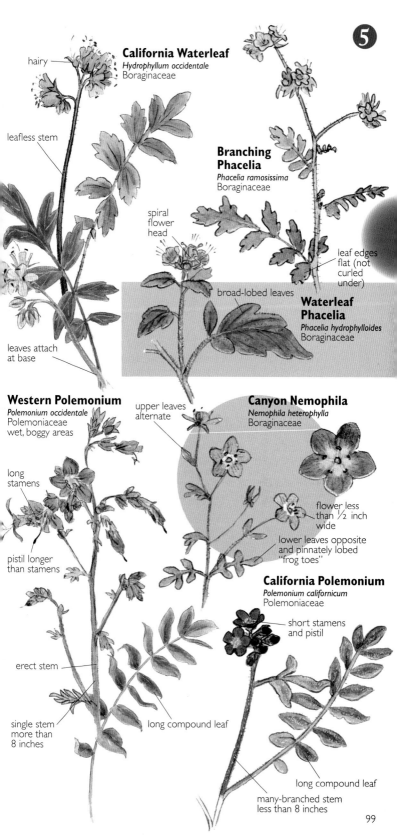

California Waterleaf
Hydrophyllum occidentale
Boraginaceae

hairy

leafless stem

Branching Phacelia
Phacelia ramosissima
Boraginaceae

spiral flower head

leaf edges flat (not curled under)

broad-lobed leaves

Waterleaf Phacelia
Phacelia hydrophylloides
Boraginaceae

leaves attach at base

Western Polemonium
Polemonium occidentale
Polemoniaceae
wet, boggy areas

upper leaves alternate

Canyon Nemophila
Nemophila heterophylla
Boraginaceae

long stamens

pistil longer than stamens

flower less than ½ inch wide

lower leaves opposite and pinnately lobed "frog toes"

California Polemonium
Polemonium californicum
Polemoniaceae

short stamens and pistil

erect stem

long compound leaf

single stem more than 8 inches

long compound leaf

many-branched stem less than 8 inches

5 Ultraviolet Patterns

Many plants have petals that are marked with lines, called nectar guides, that help direct insects to the pollen and nectar. Some plants have patterns that are invisible to the human eye but are prominent to insects that see in the ultraviolet spectrum.

Bird's Eye Gilia
Gilia tricolor
Polemoniaceae

blue anthers

purple throat

yellow tube

finely branched leaves

short stamens

thin hairless stem with narrow leaves

Lewis's Flax
Linum lewisii
Linaceae

Spreading Phlox
Phlox diffusa
Polemoniaceae
rocky areas

petal at right angle to tube

leaves opposite and not lobed or painfully sharp

variable petal color

Fiesta Flower
Pholistoma auritum
Boraginaceae
low elevation

long lobed leaves (lower leaves opposite)

long stems, shrub-like

Velvety Stickseed
Hackelia velutina
Boraginaceae

flowers larger than 3/8 inch

Hackelia flowers have raised white appendages in the center

Sierra Stickseed
Hackelia nervosa
Boraginaceae

flower more than half an inch wide

large pale center

distinct veins

flowers smaller than 3/8 inch

Baby Blue-eyes
Nemophila menziesii
Boraginaceae

hooked seeds attach to clothing and animal fur

Felwort
Swertia perennis
Gentianaceae

dark veins on white background

long petals

alternate leaves

opposite and alternate leaves

Mountain Bluebells
Mertensia ciliata
Boraginaceae

cluster of tubular flowers

Explorer's Gentian
Gentiana calycosa
Gentianaceae

deep tube with white spots at rim

opposite leaves

Purple Nightshade
Solanum xanti
Solanaceae

stamens form a yellow cone

petals pale or dark purple

small shrub

Matted Yerba Santa
Eriodictyon lobbii
Boraginaceae

smooth leaf edge

flowers grow from tip and from leaf axils

lobed leaf

Rothrock's Nama
Nama rothrockii
Boraginaceae

flowers clumped at tip

Sky Pilot
Polemonium eximium
Polemoniaceae
high alpine

fern-like leaves with musky odor

leaves at base

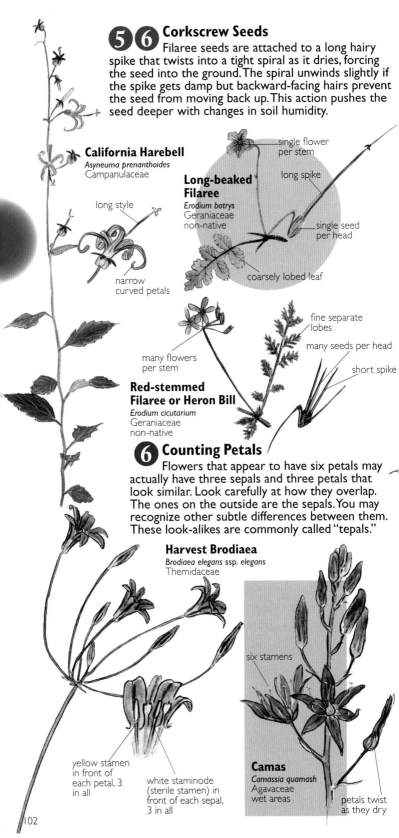

5 6 Corkscrew Seeds

Filaree seeds are attached to a long hairy spike that twists into a tight spiral as it dries, forcing the seed into the ground. The spiral unwinds slightly if the spike gets damp but backward-facing hairs prevent the seed from moving back up. This action pushes the seed deeper with changes in soil humidity.

California Harebell
Asyneuma prenanthoides
Campanulaceae

long style

narrow curved petals

Long-beaked Filaree
Erodium botrys
Geraniaceae
non-native

single flower per stem

long spike

single seed per head

coarsely lobed leaf

many flowers per stem

Red-stemmed Filaree or Heron Bill
Erodium cicutarium
Geraniaceae
non-native

fine separate lobes

many seeds per head

short spike

6 Counting Petals

Flowers that appear to have six petals may actually have three sepals and three petals that look similar. Look carefully at how they overlap. The ones on the outside are the sepals. You may recognize other subtle differences between them. These look-alikes are commonly called "tepals."

Harvest Brodiaea
Brodiaea elegans ssp. *elegans*
Themidaceae

six stamens

yellow stamen in front of each petal, 3 in all

white staminode (sterile stamen) in front of each sepal, 3 in all

Camas
Camassia quamash
Agavaceae
wet areas

petals twist as they dry

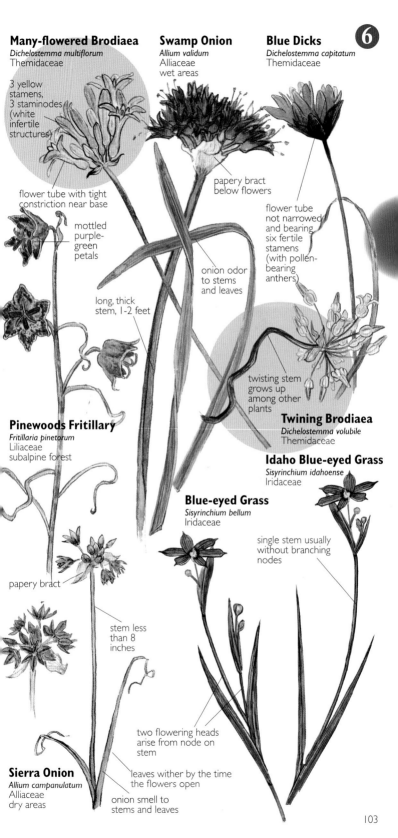

Many-flowered Brodiaea
Dichelostemma multiflorum
Themidaceae

3 yellow stamens, 3 staminodes (white infertile structures)

flower tube with tight constriction near base

mottled purple-green petals

Swamp Onion
Allium validum
Alliaceae
wet areas

papery bract below flowers

onion odor to stems and leaves

long, thick stem, 1-2 feet

Blue Dicks
Dichelostemma capitatum
Themidaceae

flower tube not narrowed and bearing six fertile stamens (with pollen-bearing anthers)

twisting stem grows up among other plants

Twining Brodiaea
Dichelostemma volubile
Themidaceae

Pinewoods Fritillary
Fritillaria pinetorum
Liliaceae
subalpine forest

papery bract

stem less than 8 inches

Idaho Blue-eyed Grass
Sisyrinchium idahoense
Iridaceae

single stem usually without branching nodes

Blue-eyed Grass
Sisyrinchium bellum
Iridaceae

two flowering heads arise from node on stem

leaves wither by the time the flowers open

onion smell to stems and leaves

Sierra Onion
Allium campanulatum
Alliaceae
dry areas

M An Identification Challenge

Many purple daisy-like flowers can be found in the Sierra. To differentiate between the asters on this page and the fleabanes on the next, look carefully at the way the phyllaries (scales under the flower) are arranged.

Asters Stems are leafy. Often without basal leaves (except *O. alpigenum*). Purple-tipped phyllaries in 3 or more rows and overlapping like shingles on a roof. Petals scraggly, few.

Fleabanes Often with a distinct clump of basal leaves. Green-tipped phyllaries in 1-2 equal rows and parallel, like a picket fence. Buds may droop. Petals robust, many.

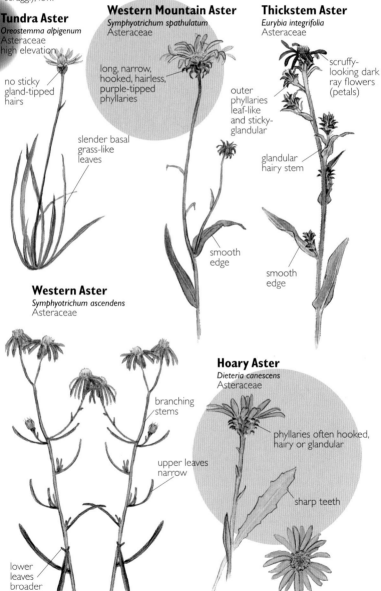

Tundra Aster
Oreostemma alpigenum
Asteraceae
high elevation

no sticky gland-tipped hairs

slender basal grass-like leaves

Western Mountain Aster
Symphyotrichum spathulatum
Asteraceae

long, narrow, hooked, hairless, purple-tipped phyllaries

smooth edge

Thickstem Aster
Eurybia integrifolia
Asteraceae

scruffy-looking dark ray flowers (petals)

outer phyllaries leaf-like and sticky-glandular

glandular hairy stem

smooth edge

Western Aster
Symphyotrichum ascendens
Asteraceae

branching stems

upper leaves narrow

lower leaves broader at tip

Hoary Aster
Dieteria canescens
Asteraceae

phyllaries often hooked, hairy or glandular

sharp teeth

Flower Clusters

A single daisy is a dense head of tiny flowers. Each yellow bump in the center is a separate flower, as is each long "petal" on the outside.

Wandering Fleabane
Erigeron glacialis
Asteraceae
above 7,000 feet

Stalked Fleabane
Erigeron algidus
Asteraceae
alpine and subalpine
above 9,500 feet

stem leaves greatly reduced or absent

leaves mostly at base

leaves on stem well developed

Chicory
Cichorium intybus
Asteraceae
non-native

fern-like leaves

Peony
Paeonia brownii
Paeoniaceae

5 sepals

drooping flowers

large pistils

basal leaves

no inner "daisy" disc

milky sap

Pygmy Fleabane
Erigeron pygmaeus
Asteraceae
high elevation

less than 2 inches

pendulous lumpy seed pods

Index

A

Canchalagua
Zeltnera venusta
Gentianaceae